D0031037

WAR AND THE
CHANGING GLOBAL SYSTEM

WAR AND THE
CHANGING GLOBAL
SYSTEM

WILLIAM K. DOMKE

Yale University Press

New Haven and London

Designed by Jo Aerne and set in
Palatino type with Univers display.
Printed in the United States of America by
BookCrafters, Inc., Chelsea, Michigan.

Library of Congress Cataloging-in-Publication Data
Domke, William Kinkade.
War and the changing global system.
Bibliography: p.
Includes index.
1. War. 2. International relations.
3. World politics—1985–1995. I. Title.
U21.2.D55   1988   355'.02   87–10577
ISBN 0–300–03689–2

*The paper in this book meets the guidelines for per-
manence and durability of the Committee on Production Guidelines for Book Longevity of the Council on Library Resources.*

10 9 8 7 6 5 4 3 2 1

To the Memory of My Parents

CONTENTS

PREFACE

No single volume can expect to provide the concluding chapters to the study of war, and I can only hope that this book moves our understanding of a selective aspect of war a bit farther down the path of knowledge. This book has two related objectives. I have first tried to advance our understanding of war by linking traditional notions of power politics to equally long-standing arguments about obstacles to war. We are well aware that decisions are taken in a limiting environment. However, studies of war rarely couple constraints to the incentives. Building on this conceptual framework, the second part of the book provides empirical investigations of the existence of constraints on decisions for war.

I was a graduate student at the University of Michigan when the underlying question of the book was framed: Has the incidence of war, which seems to occur with fairly constant frequency, been affected by the profound scope and degree of change in the global system? The exploration of this question can lead to two theoretically meaningful conclusions. If the incidence of war does not appear to be related to changes in the global system, especially those commonly and sometimes persuasively argued to limit war, then we have reason to believe that traditional power-politics perspectives are correct in understanding war as largely derivative of distributions of military power and alliance. On the other hand, if war is related to change, then we have evidence that a narrow power-politics perspective must be expanded to account more completely and systematically for the dynamic environment of governments. This is not an entirely new query, as Martin Wight framed much the same question at the outset of the postwar preoccupation with international relations: "In the study of international politics we are dogged by the insistent problem, whether the relations between Powers are in fact more than 'power politics' in the popular sense of the term, and whether they can become more" (Wight, 1946, p. 62). This, too, is the question of this book.

I would like to thank the many people who provided encouragement and assistance throughout the project. Mentors deserve special credit, and I would like to graciously thank both Harold K. Jacobson and A. F. K. Organski for their support, encouragement, and advice. I am indebted to Paul Bairoch of the University of Geneva, who was most helpful in supplying data and assistance on the data used in chapter 5. Ted Gurr's data on polity persistence were supplied by the Inter-university Consortium for Political and Social Research (Study Number 5010), which also permitted me to quote material from their codebook. Of the several readers of the manuscript, Maria Courtis, George Downs, and Jacek Kugler gave me many useful comments. Lynn Page Whittaker provided many important improvements to an early draft. Michael Joyce did an outstanding job of editing for publication. Eunice Carlson and Vickie Zinner worked hard and capably in preparing various versions. My wife, Carla Caruso, endured the whole effort and deserves special thanks.

WAR AND THE
CHANGING GLOBAL
SYSTEM

1

WAR AND
POWER POLITICS

Decisions to go to war are constrained by domestic political structure, foreign trade, and participation in international organization. Decisions for war must be understood as the product of calculated choices by national governments bounded by the limiting aspects of their environment. Although this is hardly a novel perspective on world politics, it has proven difficult to translate into meaningful theoretical arguments and productive research. Accordingly, I seek to establish in this book the degree to which changing features in the global system can be seen to constrain the ability to go to war.

Since at least the emergence of the modern state system at the end of the Thirty Years' War, no generation and few nations have been left unaffected by the occurrence of war between independent national governments.[1] Despite the persistence of interstate war,

---

1. Although the choice of terms for key concepts often seems arbitrary in the literature of international relations, it is important to be clear in meaning. Reference to the modern state system describes the evolution and practices of international relations between independent national units since the seventeenth century. The concept of an international system is ambiguous; to some it comprises properties of its own, and to others it represents merely the sum of its component national parts. I have chosen to use the term *global system* to describe the variety of economic, social, and political interactions among many types of actors because it is sufficiently general without implying any particular system attributes (see Modelski, 1978), unlike the term *world system*, which has acquired a special connotation with respect to the writings of Wallerstein and others. The principal political units in the global system are most commonly referred to as sovereign states or nation-states. I prefer *independent national governments* as a more neutral yet descriptive term. Sovereignty is an ambiguous concept, and independence, especially with respect to the operation of foreign policy, is a sufficient description of the requirement of autonomous action in world affairs (see Ruggie, 1983, pp. 273–81; also Wolfers, 1959, p. 103). The

1

not enough is understood about the causes and conditions of its onset. A large catalogue of theories and research findings exists, but there is little consensus to guide students of war to solid conclusions upon which to base theory (Singer, 1981; Eberwein, 1981). This confusion stems largely from the complex nature of world politics itself, which has stimulated a body of literature containing diverse and often contradictory notions about the causes of war.

My study is not intended to review and criticize the vast scholarly literature on war. But because a major hindrance to the accumulation of knowledge is the vague or inconsistent conceptualization of various aspects of war, it is best to start with a discussion of concepts in order that the findings I present can be evaluated in the context of other research (Fink, 1968). Although there are many obstacles to theoretical advancements, a major part of the inability to progress in the understanding of war stems from confusion about two quite distinct conceptualizations of the onset of war and, more generally, the nature of foreign-policy behavior (Sprout and Sprout, 1965; Gilpin, 1981, preface). Theories of war portray its occurrence as either the result of calculated choice by governments (volition) or the product of environmental pressures (constraint). Because both are relevant dimensions of war, adequate theory must reconcile these two sources of behavior.

The volitional perspective sees war as the product of reasoned choice by statesmen. The application of violent force is a means to an end and comes from reasoned or rational decisions by governments, if "rational" is defined as consistent with an ordered set of preferences and explicit goals. This is the view of Clausewitz, who

---

concept of national government more accurately depicts the constellation of individuals and institutions that act on behalf of a nation. This follows the useful conceptualizations found in Russett, Singer, and Small (1968). The term *state* connotes an identity of action with a single integral unit, and its use often assumes particular state-society relationships which I wish to avoid here. In short, the concept of state is as much an assumption as a description of the political institutions governing a society and interacting with other foreign actors. Since war between independent national governments is the focus of this study, further references to war are to this restricted class of conflict behavior and not to civil wars or colonial wars, which do not involve two or more independent national governments.

called attention to the instrumental nature of decisions for war. Governments are purposive and goal-directed whenever they issue a declaration of war or take direct action with force.

A volitional view of behavior assumes that individuals act to optimize valued interests, that their preferences are readily identifiable, and that the calculation of the costs of alternative action governs choice. To many this is a purely "economic" approach to the study of behavior, because the outcomes of social interaction are seen as the product of the self-interests of the component actors, whose influence is weighted by suitably defined social power (Barry, 1970). Further, the motivations behind behavior are assumed to be contained in the action itself (for example, Germany's invasion of Poland in 1939 describes its motivation to acquire additional territory). When applied to foreign policy, the volitional view presupposes that the preferences and goals of national governments are clearly defined and that actions serve only to further these well-specified interests. Constraints on choice exist as the costs of action, against which the benefits must be balanced. The clearest development of the volitional perspective comes in the form of game-theoretic analyses of foreign policy, where the desire to optimize the balance of behavioral payoffs functions to structure rational choice. Bruce Bueno de Mesquita bases his analyses of decisions for war on the "expected utility" of such action (1981), that is, governments maximize their self-interest through rational calculations of the anticipated costs and risks of war.

The contrasting environmental or sociological perspective sees war as the outcome of the interaction of complicated developments in the global system. Decisions have meaning only in the context of situational factors relevant to the outbreak of war. Changes in a nation's international position or domestic composition create situations leading to a decision for war—which is not to say that governments do not choose for themselves. Instead, environmental stimuli generate conditions conducive to war and dominate the particular preferences and goals of many actors, whose conscious or unconscious motivations cannot be aggregated into a single national interest. The configuration of inducements and constraints ultimately shape the nature of intended action or inaction. Governments, as only one of many interacting groups and institutions, are thus reactive to environmental pressures and mechanistic in taking action through war.

An environmental perspective focuses on an entire social system, which in world politics is the enormously complicated and multidimensional global system. The placement of an actor in the environment of a social system produces a combination of inducements for action and constraints. Inducements are the rewards actors are socialized to accept as the product of dominant norms and values (Barry, 1970), whereas constraints are the obstacles that hinder the pursuit of such rewards. Actors are thus subject to a combination of environmental determinants, taken selectively or cumulatively, and it is the task of the analyst to discern their relevance correctly. For example, Marx's explanation of social trends derives exclusively from an analysis of configurations of social classes, and a historical dialectic, not explicit choices by individual actors, describes the bases of behavior. In their study of late-nineteenth-century conflict, Nazli Choucri and Robert C. North (1975) summarize the environmental forces that characterized the dynamic interaction of the governments of the great powers as "lateral pressure." In their work, the pace and distribution of changing national and imperial attributes culminated in a configuration of domestic and international pressures that led to war.

The volitional and environmental perspectives are both relevant aspects of war; in other words, they represent the "willingness" and "opportunity" of governments to use force (Most and Starr, 1984, p. 405). Governments select the option of war, but they do so in an environment that predetermines some outcomes and makes others unexpected. Existing research on the causes of war fails to integrate or reconcile these two dimensions of decisions for war (Luterbacher, 1984, p. 166). In this book, I use the volitional aspects of war as a starting point, and it is assumed that governments choose war to further a valued interest. Decisions for war as "rational choices" are the units of analysis. These acts are then juxtaposed against several environmental factors that we can reasonably believe will condition choice. Accordingly, my first goal is to better conceptualize a balance of the volitional and environmental perspectives on decisions for war; the analysis of potential constraints

4

on choice can then lead to theoretical insights into the causes of war.

CONCEPTUALIZATION OF DECISIONS FOR WAR

Generalization about the varied instances of any recurring phenomenon is easiest when only a single or very few factors are used to explain a pattern of events. Even empirical investigations of war, which seek to validate broader theoretical notions, are likely to incorporate only a few variables in modeling a more abstract set of relationships. However, war is a multifaceted phenomenon, showing different images from changing angles of view, and focus on different actions generates quite different insights. Not surprisingly, a clear understanding of its causes is elusive. Generalization requires simplification, which limits theoretical abstraction and analysis. At best one can deal only with a portion of the problem, hoping to keep that segment consistent with larger theoretical questions.

The problem of simplification, or economy in theory-building, is complicated by the limited number of instances of war. From the end of the Napoleonic Wars in 1815 to the present, only sixty interstate wars have taken place, with irregular intervals of time between them.[2] Considering the variety of circumstances in which they have occurred over a long and dynamic period of the global system, these wars provide only a small number of cases to validate theories comprised of a few or many explanatory factors, which makes overriding tendencies or causal patterns difficult to discern.

Even with such a small population of cases for study, the degree of similarity between wars is a source of disagreement among scholars. Because they constitute a common behavior—the sustained

2. The Correlates of War project under the direction of J. David Singer of the University of Michigan has compiled the most complete and careful survey of the incidence of war. Their population of interstate wars is limited to the sustained use of force, defined as greater than one thousand battle deaths, between independent national governments. Conflicts between other types of political units are classified as civil or imperial wars. See Singer and Small's *Wages of War* (1972) and its revision, *The Resort to Arms* (1982). My amendments to their population of cases are discussed in chapter 3.

and violent use of force by at least two independent national governments—a strong case can be made that they can be analyzed as a single class of behavior, a distinct subset of interactions in world politics. They are not difficult to identify when they occur, and only a few criteria are necessary to distinguish a population of interstate wars from other types of conflict (see Small and Singer, 1982). On the basis of such similarities, or on other elements common to war, generalization and theory-building can take place.

No one can deny, however, that every war has a character of its own: each is fought over a particular dispute or the ambitions of a single government. Though unified by the common desire to prevail over another government, the preferences and goals of each government at war are different. Is studying war as a class of behavior an attempt to compare apples with oranges?[3]

The incidence of each war is unique in many ways, but all wars between governments share common characteristics, and these can be the focus of analysis and theory-building. In this book, the two positions are resolved by conducting the same analyses for each separate occurrence of war, which allows the particular characteristics of decisions for war to be studied in the light of broader theoretical arguments.

The need and basis of analytic comparison is nowhere better expressed than in the writings of Karl von Clausewitz (*On War*, 1832), who emphasized the ability to draw generalizable conclusions and also identified the common elements of war, in which the perspectives of volition and environment are combined. The first chapter, "What is War?" ends with a discussion of the results for theory:[4]

3. The essays in *Contending Approaches to International Politics* (1969) edited by Klaus Knorr and James Rosenau present the best delineation of positions in this debate on the potential for generalization and theory-building.

4. John Tashjean provides a useful assessment of Clausewitz in "Clausewitz: Naval and Other Considerations," pp. 51–58. Tashjean provides his own translation to the following passage: "War . . . is a total phenomenon [having] dominant tendencies [that] always make war an idiosyncratic trinity—composed of primordial violence, hatred and enmity, which are to be regarded as a blind natural force; of the play of chance and probability within which the creative spirit is free to roam; and of its element of subordination, as an instrument of policy which makes it subject to reason alone."

War is, therefore, not only chameleon-like in character, because it changes its color in some degree in each particular case, but it is also, as a whole, in relation to the predominant tendencies which are in it, a wonderful trinity, composed of the original violence of its elements, hatred and animosity, which may be looked upon as blind instinct; of the play of probabilities and chance, which make it a free activity of the soul; and of the subordinate nature of a political instrument, by which it belongs purely to the reason.

The first of these three phases concerns more the people; the second more the General and his Army; the third, more the Government. The passions that break forth in War must already have a latent existence in the peoples. The range which the display of courage and talents shall get in the realm of probabilities and of chance depends on the particular characteristics of the General and the Army, but the political objectives belong to the government alone (pp. 121–22.).

Clausewitz's statement makes clear that the combination of factors that make individual wars unique also provides a framework by which decisions for war can be compared in a systematic way. The "wonderful trinity" may be strangely titled, but the three elements are present in each occurrence of war between national governments. Together, they represent three general phases in the onset of war and a framework of elements that must be dealt with in order to provide a full understanding of war. This is no less true of an attempt to explain the incidence of a single war than of the ability to understand war as a recurring phenomenon in world affairs. To Clausewitz, the "task . . . is to develop a theory that maintains a balance between these three tendencies, like an object suspended between three magnets" (Tashjean, 1986, p. 52).

The first element—one that must logically precede the consideration of war by any government—is the existence of a dispute or rivalry. Wars are not accidents; they result from conflicting claims between governments or from territorial ambition and are fought over these particular objectives. Harold and Margaret Sprout's concept of foreign-policy behavior as "policy-contingent" action posits that choice is based on the underlying motivations: values, pref-

7

erence, moods, attitudes, perception, cognition, and recognition (1965, pp. 212–25; see also Baldwin, 1979). A decision for war is thus grounded in a set of underlying motivations related to the objectives being pursued through the use of force.

Despite this essential ingredient, however, the causes of war rest on widely divergent bases of dispute, ranging from intense disagreements over proper boundaries and nationality (the cause of the four wars in the Middle East since the creation of Israel) to clear-cut acts of territorial expansion, even if they are justified with reference to harmed interests (Hitler's invasion of Poland and the Japanese occupation of Manchuria). To conclude that a government acted to further its interests or extend its influence is inadequate but underscores the difficulty of generalizing about foreign-policy objectives.

Of course, issues in dispute are not identical with war aims or the motivations behind decisions for war, which are largely unknown, if not unconscious. Certainly, official statements or explanations of war aims cannot be trusted. In addition, motivations cannot be aggregated across individuals to form a national motivation, because each individual possesses his or her own motivation or a mixed set of motivations. Indeed, an important hypothesis holds that a decision for war requires a proliferation of motivations so that each individual decision-maker can draw upon a menu of war aims. Ernest May, for example, argues that the U.S. decision for war with Spain in 1898 and annexation of the Phillippines was facilitated by a coalition of individuals for whom these actions represented an avenue to pursue distinct ambitions (May, 1968). The issue in dispute must also be distinguished from the antecedent of war, which is an act that prompts decision-making to resolve issues in dispute. For example, the assassination of Archduke Franz Ferdinand was the antecedent of Austria-Hungary's decision to extend its dominion in the Balkans by war with Serbia, the sinking of the *Maine* the antecedent to the Spanish-American War over Cuban independence, and a soccer match the antecedent to a war over the boundaries between El Salvador and Honduras. The issue of each war is the item in dispute between governments, whereby the demands of one government are met by a denial of compliance.

Underlying disputes create the chameleon-like character of war.

Although some issues, such as the rights and boundaries of Israel, are fought over repeatedly, a broad and overlapping range of underlying disputes exists, and historians differ widely on the objectives of and interpretations by governments in many wars. Lewis Fry Richardson's pioneering study (1960), for example, used a broad definition of war and examined economic, linguistic, and religious differences as factors in conflicts. Although present in some degree, none of these underlying factors emerge as common reasons for war. Disputes over territory are frequent and seem consistent with the desire of nations to expand, but they are most often questions of nationality and the legitimacy of competing national governments, not purely attempts at territorial expansion.

A recent compendium listing seventy contemporary cases of border and territorial disputes (Day, 1982) sheds further light on the difficulty of connecting the nature of disputes to war. Defined as actively contested (no permanent settlement has been reached), eighteen of these disputes have been fought over during a war included in this book. In the 1980s, boundary disputes have led to wars between Iran and Iraq, China and Vietnam, and Argentina and the United Kingdom. The Western Sahara, Chad, East Timor, and the Soviet-Chinese border have been the scenes of lower forms of conflict. But why have the other territorial disputes remained benign? Clearly, knowledge of the nature of the dispute itself is insufficient to explain why some disputes lead to war and others do not.

The environmental view of war posits that disputes leading to war are generated by patterns of interaction in the global system. Governments can react to conflict and challenges only as they arise. Disputes between nations emerge from dynamic and extremely diverse interactions between societies, and it is not often that governments can select at will the issues over which discord will occur. The disputes, to Clausewitz, are "of the people," and no government can easily regulate the animosities and interactions of an entire nation. This point seems self-evident, for many disputes between governments arise out of proper or improper acts of citizens; U.S. Marines have often been sent ashore to rescue errant Americans from foreign governments, and diplomatic challenges and protests of harm are almost too numerous to count. Most important,

9

not all governments can skillfully manage the animosities arising from ethnic conflict that generate intense rivalries between populations. Governments thus have only limited abilities to deal selectively with the disputes that motivate war.

The volitional view, in contrast, emphasizes that governmental actions may be the source of disputes leading to war. Whatever the balance of cooperative and conflictual interaction between nations, a government must judge particular disputes as potential situations for the use of force. Indeed, governments may find special opportunities arising from events over which they had no control. Although disputes may spring from the environment, governments must still choose whether or not to ignore them or escalate to a contest of demands. Other forms of action or inaction may also produce desirable results.

The second set of considerations is Clausewitz's "play of probabilities and chance": the prospects of success in the use of force. This element rests on the perceived capabilities of the governments involved. Given the occurrence of a dispute, governments will act with force only when they determine (with or without the consent of the military) that the chance for success is sufficiently favorable.

An extensive literature supports the proposition that national governments are more likely to use force when they perceive an acceptable chance of success. Bruce Bueno de Mesquita's recent work on expected utility and decisions for war shows that governments exhibit a consistent and robust tendency to choose war only when they perceive an advantage in military capability and the attending risk to be acceptable (1981, 1985). In many respects, Bueno de Mesquita's analyses are a direct investigation of the play of probabilities and chance.[5] Other things being equal, governments do

5. Bueno de Mesquita analyzes decisions for war using a model of expected utility based on the combination of capability, uncertainty, and risk. I attribute his findings to Clausewitz's second element, although consideration of uncertainty and risk may be construed as a part of the third element, governmental choice. Since his model does not take into account the objectives of war as an instrument of policy, I restrict the meaning of his findings to the play of probabilities and chance. In addition, since Bueno de Mesquita operationalizes uncertainty and risk on the basis of alliance relationships, his model represents a more complete investigation of the factors relevant to the calculation of probable success (see Wagner, 1984). Moreover, Bueno de Mesquita recognizes this point

choose force when they anticipate it will succeed, but this optimism must of course be true of both parties (Snyder and Diesing, 1977, p. 193).

War as an instrument, the volitional view of war, is the key to the second element of this framework. The play of probabilities and chance refers to a reasoned assessment of the prospects for success in achieving an objective, after the opportunity to use force arises. When governments estimate their chances to employ force to their advantage, we are viewing decision-makers guided by a sense of free will. Whether they are good performers at estimating prospects of success is not at question, only whether they act on the basis of the expectation that the war will succeed in accomplishing a desired end. The difficulty in correctly establishing the probability of success transforms the fortunes of war into ruinous folly.

The play of probabilities and chance also includes an environmental aspect, because governments have access to only limited power resources. Governments can do a great deal to prepare for war, but their power is largely determined by their nation's demographic size and composition, economic resources, and political organization. Geographical and resource vulnerabilities can be compensated for through alliance and other measures, but no government has the ability to generate power capabilities at will because it is bounded by the environmental constraint of limited resources.[6] Governments also face the uncertainty and risk associated with actions taken by allies and adversaries.

The third element of war is the decision itself, the political choice to use force as an instrument of policy. If we observe that there is some contested issue of dispute in any war and we agree with Bueno de Mesquita's analysis that decisions for war are taken with an expectation that force will succeed, then we are left with the question of why all disputes in which the play of probabilities favors resort to force do not result in war. The expectation of success

---

when he emphasizes that his findings represent necessary and not sufficient conditions for war.

6. There is a large literature on the relevant components of power as an attribute. Organski and Kugler review the major alternatives and present measurements in *The War Ledger* (1980). See also Kugler and Domke, "The Strength of Nations" (1986).

is a necessary but not sufficient condition for war to occur. Crisis bargaining and alternative settlement of the issue in dispute can also play a determining role (Leng and Gochman, 1982; Leng, 1983).

The formulation of national policy and the matching of means to ends constitute the most complicated element of war. Like other decision-making processes, decisions on war involve interpersonal relationships between political elites, competing positions of influential interest groups in society, and variable perceptions of other governments' intentions. In the end, decisions for war are the outcome of an ordered or disordered balancing of inducements against constraints. As an act of policy, unlike the generation of dispute and the calculation of prospects, any decision for war requires an agreement or dominating position among controlling political elites. Within government, disagreement on the objectives in dispute and chances of success can differ.

Volition obviously plays a large role in this process. Only an independent government in the global system can decide, on the basis of objectives and prospects for success, which disputes require force (high stakes), which can be dealt with short of force (low stakes), and which can be ignored or treated as little more than a nuisance (no stakes). Governments, or rather political elites that dominate, must choose whether and how to act.

But governments cannot always control their menu of options, because other actors, both foreign and domestic, can demand policies or acts to constrain freedom of choice. In many instances, including the British entry into both world wars or the Soviet invasion of Finland in 1939, governments asserted that they had no choice but to resort to force. And Arnold Wolfers compared governments acting under pressure to "a house on fire"—members of an audience may react differently to changes in temperature, but when "fire" is yelled, all will flee (1959, p. 94). In short, the decision-making environment is most often a cramped one, since the degree of environmental constraint and socialization limits the possibility to exercise governmental choice, especially if actions are seen as the result of compromise among a constellation of governmental or domestic political actors.

A decision for war is not the unbounded exercise of governmental will, nor is it dictated solely by circumstances. It is the manifestation of the same decision processes that generate all governmental policies; the volitional and environmental dimensions combine in a government's choice to go to war or not. The element of governmental decision-making couples the calculating will and purpose of government to the panoply of forces in society and the world that limit or guide nations toward or away from war.

Taken together, the three elements of war and the two perspectives on the source of behavior in international relations provide a more complete conceptualization of decisions for war. The elements delineate separate stages, or considerations, of decisions for war, while the two theoretical perspectives on behavior provide insight on the factors pertinent to each element. They can be summarized as follows:

THEORETICAL PERSPECTIVES ON BEHAVIOR

Element of War	Volition	Environment
Dispute "Hatred and animosity"	Selection of disputes for potential escalation	Sum of cooperative and conflictual relationships
Capability "Play of probabilities and chance"	Calculation of prospects for success	Distribution of relevant power resources
Choice "a political instrument"	Governmental decision for war as an act of political will	Inducements and constraints

From a purely volitional perspective, the conceptualization of decisions for war centers on the initiative and calculations of governments. First, governments, on whatever basis, decide on their objectives. They may choose to expand or maintain national wealth through the acquisition of territory or, more limitedly, to resolve an ambiguous boundary dispute or a question of legal status. No matter what the substance of the dispute, a government may ponder the pursuit of a particular objective with force. Second, a government then calculates whether it has the military capability to succeed on the battlefield, which may partly depend on the anticipated support of its own allies or those of the adversary. Third, force will be applied if a government finds that the means match the end: if the use of force will have a high probability of success in accomplishing its objectives, war will ensue if the adversary resists, based on its objectives, calculations, and choice. In the absence of an environmental dimension, a simple formula results: a government wants something, believes it can take it, and decides to use force if it is not given.

Conversely, the conceptualization of war from the environmental perspective places governments in the back seat. First, disputes arise out of the interaction of societies, and governments cannot select issues of disagreement with other governments. Instead, the pretexts for war present themselves as conflicts latent in the relationships among nations. Second, governments have only limited resources to deal with these disputes, and their ability to calculate the play of probabilities and chance is even more limited by the power of opponents and actions of third parties (they may even possess restricted control over their own military establishments). Third, an environmental perspective views decisions for war as a result of external pressures that lead nations into war. Political elites are not directly responsible if the constellation of determining factors guides decision-making to an outcome of war because societal demands and the actions of others make governmental choice irrelevant. On the other hand, if other actors or considerations constrain governmental action, then a decision for war is not possible. In the absence of volition, wars occur as the product of social forces, which generate conflicts between societies and can translate disputes into open warfare.

These two perspectives describe different processes that, in each instance, can lead to war; but they also delineate two dimensions of the same phenomena and must be taken into account to provide a complete explanation of decisions for war—a monumental task for any single study. As noted earlier, to advance knowledge about the causes of war, it is necessary to focus research on components of the larger problem, keeping more specific questions in relation to broader theoretical issues. This conceptualization of decisions for war assists theory-building by better specifying the dimensions and elements of war. More importantly, such a framework better allows the work of other scholars to support assumptions and analyses.

Accordingly, this study focuses only on the third element of war, governmental choice. Here, it is assumed that political elites know their objectives in making decisions for war, whether they have disputes forced upon them or whether they choose for themselves. The ambiguous correlation between motivations and behavior makes this the most difficult element of war. To investigate the nature of war aims and dispute is a very different research question: what kinds of social relationships (interpersonal, intersocietal, or intergovernmental) generate conflicts that are likely to lead to war? Although the issue of disputes is analyzed in chapter 4, a full investigation of this question is far beyond the scope of this book.

It is also assumed that when governments decide for war, they believe that they will succeed, using their own military capabilities or the assistance of allies. To analyze the play of probabilities and chance is to investigate the components of power in international politics and whether governments can or do properly calculate prospects for success (see Organski and Kugler, 1980; Bueno de Mesquita, 1981). Here, the findings of previous research support theoretical arguments.

This book examines the nature of constraints that limit decisions for war. Important assumptions and observations are drawn from the literature of power politics and taken as a starting point for analysis of decisions for war. Power politics supplies the volitional dimension. Constraints on governments are then examined in order to better define the environmental factors that limit choice.

POWER POLITICS AND WAR

The power-politics conceptualization of war assumes that governments choose force as a particular means to a particular end or, at the very least, as the best available alternative. To choose war, a government must abandon reliance on other avenues to settle disputes and other methods short of war to achieve a desired objective. To choose war is to believe that coercive force is preferred to diplomacy, persuasion, and tacit-bargaining (see Downs and Rocke, 1987), that the employment of the military resources available to a government—power—will advance its interests beyond other means of influence. In the study of world poli-

the use and threat of force against other governments is called power politics.

The lore of power politics is difficult to deny.[7] At its core, it is the recognition that force is often used in world politics, while to many, it is a synonym for international politics, and the "struggle for power" is a common summary definition of the field (see Wight, 1946; Morgenthau, 1948). To some, it is the "realist" perspective, because it emphasizes the harsh realities of survival in international politics.[8] Too many independent governments have been vanquished by the force of a rival to pretend that a key element in the understanding of world affairs is not the struggle for power, defined as survival.

Power politics is also the traditional view,[9] for depiction of international politics as the struggle for survival has a long standing. Its roots can be traced to Thucydides in the fifth century B.C. His portrayal of the Athenian response to the Melian plea for peace is a cogent description of power politics: "the standard of justice depends on the equality of power to compel and that, in fact, the strong do what they have the power to do and the weak accept what they have to accept" (p. 402).[10] In other words, "might makes

7. The *American Heritage Dictionary* (Boston, 1969) defines lore as "accumulated fact, tradition, and belief about a particular subject." Because power politics is more than analytic perspective but also much less than a theory, this definition seems a more appropriate description for a body of literature concerning the use of force in world politics.

8. I use the term *power politics* to describe a set of behaviors associated with the use of force in world politics. The term *realism* has a broader connotation; in particular, it implies assumptions about human behavior that are not essential to theories built around notions of power politics. Further, the term *balance of power* is often used as a synonym for power politics. Here, *power politics* refers to concepts and principles pertaining to national foreign policy, whereas *balance of power* describes a system of interaction among governments resulting from the application of the explicit operating rules of power politics. The best treatment of the different meanings of *balance of power* is still Haas, "The Balance of Power: Prescription, Concept of Propaganda" (1953).

9. Some have gone so far as to label it the dominant paradigm in the study of world politics. See, for example, Lijphart (1974) and Mansbach and Vasquez (1981).

10. A variant translation can be found in the Modern Library edition: "right, as the world goes, is only in question between equals in power, while the strong do what they can and the weak suffer what they must" (New York, 1951, p. 331).

16

right," and the use of force is justified by the interests of the powerful. Further, this principle of behavior is fundamental to interactions among independent governments. Thucydides, through the voice of the Athenians, reports:

our knowledge of men leads us to conclude that it is a general and necessary law of nature to rule wherever one can. This is not a law that we made ourselves, nor were we the first to act upon it when it was made. We found it already in existence, and we shall leave it to exist for ever among those who come after us. We are merely acting in accordance with it, and we know that you or anybody else with the same power as ours would be acting the same way (p. 403).

The lore of power politics is echoed in the countless writings of observers and scholars who find the desire to extend power, even if only vaguely defined, to be a sufficient explanation for the use of force. The principles of power politics are largely taken as a given property of world politics by political philosophers, although many identified and supported methods for its demise, among them Machiavelli, whose name is popularly associated with "might makes right." Hobbes's *Leviathan* ([1651] 1946) contains a reference to the state system as an example of the brutish "state of nature": "In all time, Kings, and Persons of Soveraigne authority, because of their independency, are in continual jealousies, and in the state and posture of Gladiators; having their weapons pointing, and their eyes fixed on one another; frontiers of their kingdomes; and continual spyes upon their neighbours; which is a posture of war" (pp. 187–88). Over the centuries, scholars have taken power politics either as an unavoidable characteristic of world politics or, more often, as a tendency that must be subdued in some way to avoid the calamaties of war.[11]

In the twentieth century, several prominent scholars have promoted the concepts and importance of power politics as a way to

11. Discussions of the nature of power politics in political philosophy are too numerous to review here. Friedrich Meinecke's *Machiavellism: The Doctrine of Raison d'Etat and Its Place in Modern History* (1957), Carr's *Twenty Years' Crisis* (1939), and Kenneth Waltz's *Man, the State, and War* (1959), review much of the relevant literature.

17

understand otherwise complicated international interactions. Although many scholars can be located in the power-politics school, E. H. Carr stands out for his timely and persuasive exposition of the role of power in world politics. In *The Twenty Years' Crisis*, written in the summer of 1939 and published in the month after Germany's invasion of Poland, Carr sets out the need to balance utopian idealism with a recognition of the "realist" perspective and the central role of power and war in relations among governments: "The supreme importance of the military instrument lies in the fact that the *ultima ratio* of power in international relations is war, not as a desirable weapon, but as a weapon which it may require in the last resort to use" (p. 109). Carr concludes that understanding the multifaceted nature of international relations is complicated by the aspirations of harmony and prosperity expressed in utopian ideals but that, in the end, such hopes are dominated by the realities of power and the tendency of governments to use it to advance their interests. Like Clausewitz, Carr also recognized that war was only one option for governments seeking to influence others. But while governments swayed by utopian ideals may believe the possibility of war to have vanished, Carr warned, they are blind to the existence of other governments that do not share their pacifistic intentions.

The historical record is also frequently cited to buttress the doctrine of "might makes right." For example, Martin Wight (1946), a chronicler of the key concepts of power politics, and Hans Morgenthau (1948), who extended these notions to a theory of international relations, use historical examples to demonstrate the validity of the notion of power politics, and proof is found not so much in the logic of their arguments or in mere assertion as in the presentation of numerous historical cases that depict the operating principles of life in the global system based on the struggle for power. Political philosophy and history are thus combined to substantiate the relevance of power politics.

The lore of power politics is also rich in concepts that describe developments in the global system, most importantly that of independent government—the state. Power politics depicts a world of interaction between independent national governments, and although other actors operate in the global system, their activities are subordinate to the "national interests" of independent governments (Waltz, 1979, pp. 93–97). When differences emerge, the national interest will dominate firms, private groups, subnational governments, and transnational organizations.

Because no higher authority—no world government, in particular—exists, each independent government is left to its own devices to protect its independence. So long as the "strong do what they have the power to do and the weak accept what they have to accept," survival is the priority of every independent government. For the powerful (great powers), security is enhanced when there are few others stronger or as strong, whereas the weak (small powers) are left to be compliant and to hope their security can be protected by competition among the strong.

A power-politics perspective makes it possible to see the quest for security as limiting opportunities for cooperation: fear of losing power resources relative to potential rivals may preclude cooperation. Kenneth Waltz succinctly describes the difficulties of collaboration in an anarchic global system:

In a self-help system each of the units spends a portion of its effort, not forwarding its own good, but in providing the means of protecting itself against others. . . . When faced with the possibility of cooperating for mutual gain, states that feel insecure must ask how the gain will be divided. . . . Even the prospect of large absolute gains for both parties does not elicit their cooperation so long as each fears how the other will use its increased capabilities. . . . The condition of insecurity—at least the uncertainty of each about the other's future intentions and actions—works against their cooperation (1979, p. 105).

Security interests (in truth, insecurity) thus override international relations that may bring greater well-being in the form of wealth or social benefits.

Power politics describes a world of autonomous actors stratified according to relative power, which means the ability to force one's will on another through threat or use of military capability.[12] For

12. To wield influence with non-military capabilities complicates notions of

each, then, the motivation for action lies in survival, which in turn is dependent on power. Accordingly, each government will act to extend its power as a means of better insuring its security, albeit at the expense of other nations, which results in a security dilemma: the improvement of any government's security is an enhancement of its power and, by necessity, a threat to the security of other nations (see Jervis, 1976, pp. 62–76). As long as the global system is structured solely by the interactions of independent national governments, nothing can alter the prominence of power politics.

As each nation acts according to its interests, defined as the enhancement of its own security (power), wars occasionally occur to both protect and extend the resources of power. Martin Wight states flatly that "the causes of war are inherent in power politics" (1946, p. 35); wars will occur as extensions of disputes over power resources, and wars over annexation of territory and colonial expansion are consistent with the drive for more power and security.

Moreover, this description of a cruel and violent system of international politics posits that the greatest danger to survival is the emergence of a hegemon or dominant power—a government capable of jeopardizing the survival of all other independent units. Such challenges lead to general war among great powers and, as a result, to a reordering of the distribution of power capabilities (Gilpin, 1981; Modelski, 1978). Hegemony is an old concept in power politics; Thucydides, after all, was describing a Hellenic world challenged by the dominance of Athens and eventually conquered by the neighboring Macedonians. Martin Wight drew particular attention to the frequency of drives for hegemony: "The most conspicuous theme in international history is not the growth of internationalism. It is the series of efforts, by one power after another, to gain mastery of the states-system—efforts that have been defeated only by a coalition of the majority of other powers at the cost of an exhausting general war" (1978, p. 30).

Although this is only a brief review of the basic tenets of power

power politics beyond its conceptual domain. Power other than the capability to use force effectively makes the identification of power far too ambiguous. Further, the association of security with preservation of independence assumes that sufficient military capability can deal with all threats to security. On the power "fungibility" issue, see Keohane (1983, pp. 521–26).

politics and the world it describes, it is enough to call attention to the enduring presence of these concepts. Power politics earns its label as the traditional perspective on international relations by tracing consistent arguments over many centuries. Its recognition of the tendency toward the use of force by governments, which is evident in every period, enhances its relevance. The question remains, however, as to how power politics guides decisions for war. But can the power-politics conceptualization of war help build a theory of decisions for war?

With respect to the disputes underlying decisions for war, power politics does not recognize a diversity of motivations, only the variable capability to take action in pursuit of the common goal of power. As long as survival is in question, enhanced power is the dominant objective of governmental action. In an environment of anarchy, fear of others requires actions to prevent domination by other governments. If politics is the struggle for power, decisions for war must be understood as part of any government's attempt to preserve or extend what power it has in the hope that greater power will allay fears of challenge. In an anarchical system composed of independent governments, the "hatred and animosities of the people" are of far less concern than the threat posed by rival governments.

This singularity of motives for war is an attractive aspect of power politics. Motivational aspects of international politics are the most troublesome to discern, and power-politics notions solve these problems by reducing the objectives of governments to the drive for security or, phrased differently, the fear of others. Further, the use of force is an important, even necessary, tool to guard and enhance it. Power politics solves the confusing chameleon-like character of war by assuming that the peculiarities of disputes are subsumed under the rubric of the struggle for power; the *casus belli* of any war is its antecedent and not its objective. Although vague and unsatisfying to followers of Clausewitz, who wish to know the more tangible objectives of military action, such an assumption permits generalization about all wars.

If the security dilemma characterizes all governmental interests, then the relevant feature of the environment becomes the distribution of military capability. Accordingly, power politics is directly relevant to the play of probabilities and chance. If survival is the permanent and dominant goal of governmental action, then governments must constantly calculate (volition) their position (the environment) with respect to rivals and potential hegemons. In decisions for war, one can almost hear Thucydides' words declaring that the "strong do what they have the power to do," mostly to the weak. And, following the work of Bueno de Mesquita (1981, 1985), governments do act when they calculate a favorable "expected utility" in the use of force against others.

The economic dimension of international relations is critical because interests defined in terms of security and military capability are closely connected to economic resources and access to wealth. Power must be created from a pool of societal or imperial resources, and the pursuit of security and the pursuit of wealth cannot be separated (Modelski, 1978; Gilpin, 1981; also McNeil, 1982). To be economically dominant is to be politically dominant, as the terms *Pax Britannica* and *Pax Americana* suggest. Lack of access to strategic materials is a vulnerability that erodes military capability and power.

What then of a government's choice for war, the third element of war? If diverse objectives are reduced to the drive for power and we accept the observation that governments act only when they anticipate success, it is still necessary to explain why the choice for war is made. Theories of international relations based on power politics use the distribution of power among great powers—the structure of the system—to account for the actions of government and explain decisions for war as the product of a government's response to threats to its place in the structure of the system and the opportunities available to improve its security position, even to the point of hegemony. Decisions for war are characterized by a means-ends formula: power or security can be improved through the use of force with reasonable certainty. Wars are categorized as (1) imperialistic, if a government exploits a threat of opportunity to expand power, (2) anti-imperialistic, if another government resists expansion, or (3) preventative, if a government finds an opportunity to stop the growing power of a rival (Morgenthau, 1948, pp. 229–30). The volitional and environmental perspectives are combined by identifying the objective of action as the pursuit of power and restricting the relevant environmental factors to the distribution of power capabilities: if expansion of power is possible, it is attempted.

In the flowering of theory-building in international relations since 1945, many theories have been put forward, some of which are more wedded to power politics than others. A prominent and clear, almost classical theory of international relations was offered by Hans Morgenthau in 1948 (see especially chaps. 11–14). In the struggle for power in the international system—or any other anarchic social system, for that matter—nations must form coalitions to resist the challenge of hegemony by a single nation seeking world empire. This generates a balance of power, which is the natural outgrowth of the pursuit of greater security. In its purist form, the actions of governments are dictated by the logic of the distribution of power in the international system. To Morgenthau, particular configurations of power capabilities require a particular response by each great-power government (small powers being largely irrelevant). A potential hegemon must be met by an alliance of lesser powers; a dominating coalition must be balanced by a countervailing coalition. War is called for when ambitions and fears produce the test of wills leading to a potential domination or a restored balance. In short, the structure of the system—as defined in the distribution of power of nations and their alliances—creates both the incentives for war and the constraints on governmental choice.

BEYOND POWER POLITICS

Since Morgenthau presented his theory, many challenges, refinements, and variations have been proposed (in particular, Waltz, 1979). But, theories of international relations based on power politics share common characteristics. Robert Keohane, in reviewing theories he labels "structural realism," finds three assumptions common to modern theories derived from power politics: (1) states are the most important actors in world politics, (2) states seek power, and (3) states carefully calculate costs of alternative policies and act to maximize "expected utility" (1983, pp. 506–12). However, what Keohane calls assumptions are better identified as generalizing simplifications or abstractions that limit the

23

extent to which theories can deal with the variability in three elements of foreign policy: actors, interests, and alternative avenues of international interaction.

A particularly troublesome simplification is the exclusive focus on integral sovereign states whose national governments are the only units capable of going to war, even though (1) all governments are comprised of many groups, factions, and organizations, (2) state-society relations—domestic political structures—necessitate that actions be compatible with the requirements of legitimacy and rule, and (3) numerous transnational actors operate in the global system. This state-centric orientation—what Arnold Wolfers called the "billiard-ball" model of homogeneous units (1959, pp. 100–105)—reduces the environmental factors in decision-making to the restricted set of features pertaining to the distribution of power capabilities among independent national governments.

This simplification is a useful abstraction for the building of theory because it reduces a complicated decision-making setting to an intellectually manageable size (see Wolfers, 1959, pp. 92–94). If world politics is confusing and the security of governments is frequently challenged then it is reasonable to assume that decision-makers are guided by the logic of the distribution of power in the system. The primacy of security calls attention to the direct threat to that security—other nations' power—and given the restricted cognitive abilities of decision-makers, it may be that decision-makers in all governments are guided solely by the structure of the system defined by the distribution of power. Confining world politics to states is thus an important and potentially valid abstraction, but only if it is a cognitive necessity for all ruling elites, who find environment too complicated to understand subtly. Variation in the quality of statesmanship, however, suggests that this is unlikely.

Theories derived from power politics must also assume that the pursuit of power is the dominant interest of independent governments. In the international anarchy, survival as an independent actor requires that security remains paramount as the goal of foreign policy. By creating a simple agenda for action, this assumption eliminates the policy-contingent or chameleon-like character of war, as each use of force is presumed to be based on the security needs of the nation. The issue in each war, and the underlying motivation, is increased or preserved security.

To assert a common motivation for war permits far greater theoretical generality. However, this level of abstraction cannot easily account for other values or objectives of government, especially when security and power are defined ambiguously. It is possible, for example, to assert that economic gain cannot be separated from power and security, but the diversity of economic actors in a national economy makes it difficult to see how any action to enhance security, especially war, can exclusively promote gains and not impose significant losses on some economic actors, be they firms, banks, farmers, consumers, or taxpayers. In short, a balance of interests lies behind any governmental action. Security interests may dominate in an act of war, but other interests may constrain and remove that option in other instances.

The emphasis on survival and the power to protect it further restricts behavior as to the use of threat or force. After all, the distribution of military capability, including alliance, defines the structure of the international system. Power politics ignores other avenues and behaviors in relations between governments that may have direct bearing on security.

Despite the limitation of theories, power politics provides important insights. From the perspective of unqualified power politics, decisions for war stem exclusively from the play of probabilities and chance. The logic of the distribution of power, seen as the ability to dominate or resist domination, governs choice. A government that finds its military capabilities diminished can soon expect a challenge from a more powerful government and should do what it can to expand its capabilities on its own or in alliance with others. Otherwise, a more powerful rival government, in its calculation of prospects for success in the use of force, will threaten the security and independence of the weaker. Further, if non-governmental actors (corporations, religions, interest groups and organizations) could use force against governments, contrary to Keohane's requirement of a state-centric assumption, they could easily be understood in a power-politics perspective. After all, the diversity of actors in premodern times was accommodated by the lore of power politics.

It is possible that the relevance of power politics stems not from the realities of the international system but from a process of socialization. The lore of power politics has many persuasive aspects, especially in its most popular presentations. Have ruling elites been socialized into its norms and the use of force over the course of time? This seems unlikely, since it would then be difficult to ignore wide variation in socialization, which would stand out as deviance from recognized diplomatic practice. Harold Nicolson, the twentieth century's most prominent diplomatic observer, criticized the destabilizing aspects of Wilsonian Diplomacy: "When the Americans arrived as the dominant partners in the coalition, they brought with them their distrust of diplomacy, and their missionary faith in the equality of man. President Wilson was an idealist and, what was more dangerous, a consummate master of English prose" (1954, p. 84). With regard to Soviet international relations, Nicolson observed: "Their activity in foreign countries or at traditional conferences is formidable, disturbing, compulsive. I do not for one moment underestimate either its potency or its danger. But it is not diplomacy: it is something else" (1954, p. 90).

My analysis of decisions for war takes power politics as the starting point. Governments are assumed to choose war as an instrument either to accomplish a particular objective or, more simply, to expand power; further, they are assumed to embark on war only when they determine that the use of force will succeed in attaining a specified goal at an acceptable cost and risk. Finally, the structure of the system—defined as the distribution of power capabilities—is assumed to provide a major source of environmental opportunities and limitations.

Beyond power politics, however, lie other factors that may be just as critical to decisions for war. Governments take action in an environment complicated by internal pressures, which may limit a government's freedom of action, and external relationships, which may create incentives to abandon the logic of power politics in favor of other more valued interests. In short, are there constraints on governments' decisions for war other than the distribution of military capability? If there are, theories of decisions for war must look beyond the struggle for power and survival and integrate other environmental factors.

2

CONSTRAINTS ON
DECISIONS FOR WAR

Despite the durability of the lore of power politics, the global system has undergone radical and increasingly accelerated change over the centuries. War between independent national governments persists, but time has significantly altered the nature of government and the relationships between them. Regardless of whether notions of power politics were ever fully adequate, change in the global system has also altered the power-political foundation of decisions for war. As the world has modernized and become more complicated, governments contemplating war have become subject to new potential constraints.

The impact of change has not been lost on scholars and statesmen, and to many the relevance of power politics has diminished over time.[1] Even advocates of power politics recognize that new conditions have complicated the practice of traditional diplomacy based on the use of force. In a 1978 interview, Henry Kissinger noted four reasons why policy based on "pure" power politics has become, since the era of Bismarck, the most difficult foreign policy to conduct:

It requires, first of all, a constantly correct assessment of the elements of power. Secondly, it demands a total ruthlessness and means that statesmen must be able to ignore friendship, loyalty, and anything other than the national interest. Third, it requires a domestic structure that will tolerate if not

1. Recent examples are Keohane and Nye (1977), who see the rise of "complex interdependence" as a challenge to power politics, and Morse (1976), who argues that world politics has been transformed from its classical power-politics roots. Craig and George (1983) describe how diplomacy and the use of force have been limited by domestic political economic constraints on governments over the past two centuries.

support this strategy. Fourth, it requires the absence of both permanent friends and permanent enemies, because as soon as a permanent enemy exists, freedom of maneuver is immediately reduced (1978, p. 7).

Throughout his writings, Kissinger unambiguously prescribes power politics as practiced in earlier centuries as the proper foreign-policy orientation because it best provides security—which is any nation's most valued interest. But he also notes the growing obstacles to a government that seeks to follow such principles. Kissinger's first requirement of correct power assessment points to a problem of internal consistency within power politics. Even though governments struggle for power, it is never entirely clear that power is a single attribute and by what criteria it can be assessed (Haas, 1953).

Kissinger's second requirement points to a constraint on a government's use of force: the key to successful power politics policy is acting in the "national interest." Since power politics specifies that national interest is defined in terms of security, other interests—such as economic gain or global human rights—have only subordinate or derivative relation to foreign policy. Kissinger's third requirement points to the domestic political setting of decisions for war: power politics precludes constraints produced by a society that might pose obstacles to the use of force. Flexibility of action is Kissinger's fourth requirement. Governments must anticipate potential threats from all others, whether in the short run or distant future; today's ally may be tomorrow's enemy.

The constraints on decisions for war reflect the limitations of theories based on power politics. First, the domestic structure of each independent nation is directly relevant to decisions for war; the "billiard-ball" analogy, the interaction of closed, impermeable, undifferentiated units, is a simplification that overlooks the ability of domestic actors to determine policy (Wolfers, 1959). Second, security interests are often ambiguous and sometimes disputed; a variety of preferences may guide national policy, especially if economic interests dominate it. Third, force is only one means to pursue foreign-policy goals; permanent bonds in the form of international organization can provide alternative avenues to resolve disputes.

The challenge of domestic structure is direct. If separate and different preferences exist in government, can its choice for war be understood as following a single "national interest"? Indeed, the requirements for staying in office may be so restrictive as to preclude a decision for war (the severe limitations on policy in the Swiss confederation are an extreme case). Is neutrality the product of a consensus for peace or of a configuration of autonomous political actors and institutions that make any action unlikely? Power politics suggests that decision-making is authoritarian in the sense that a dominant leader or a cohesive group of statesmen can readily agree on the national interest and the actions required to further it. But the growth of democratic institutions and greater political participation challenges this assumption.

The most potent challenge to the primacy of security is the pursuit of prosperity.[2] Power versus plenty is often referred to as a tradeoff in foreign policy (Viner, 1948). According to classical liberal thought, if nations become more involved in the mutual gain of economic exchange, security interests will be replaced by economic interests, and the national interest will be defined as the search for wealth and not as the struggle for power. At a minimum, greater commitment to foreign trade will constrain decisions for war, if a government must balance the costs of losing tangible trade profits against a gain in the ambiguous goal of security.

Flexibility of action requires traditional forms of diplomacy with its emphasis on secrecy, discretion, and even deceit, but permanent antagonisms or alignments undermine this flexibility. And although permanent antagonism is consistent with power politics, bonds of cooperation are not. Participation in and commitment to international governmental organizations (IGOs) as institutions for the management of relations in a collaborative setting encroach on

2. From a power-politics perspective, power and wealth are complementary pursuits and cannot be easily separated (see Gilpin, 1975, and Keohane, 1984). However, the separation of security and economic interests has been contested since the rise of liberal thought and the challenge to mercantilist doctrines that are consistent with power politics.

29

governmental freedom of maneuver. If governments derive greater benefits from participation in collaborative management of relations, then they are constrained in their willingness, and perhaps in their ability, to manipulate their partners by force.

These three constraints—non-security interests, domestic structure, and permanent bonds—represent a potent limitation to the understanding of decisions for war through notions of power politics. Kissinger argues that governments must avoid or override these constraints to produce better foreign policy, but the scholar must ascertain whether and to what extent these constraints condition decisions for war. Does domestic structure constrain choice? Does involvement in foreign trade create interests that limit the struggle for power? Are governments less likely to decide for war if they are otherwise committed to participation in international organizations?

DOMESTIC STRUCTURE AND WAR

The composition of the national units that form the key actors in world politics and the behavioral agents of war is as varied as the number of nations. The balance of similarities and differences is useful for cross-national comparisons, but also problematic for drawing generalizable conclusions. What elements in the domestic structure of a nation have a bearing on its government's external relations? Power politics suggests that, given the security prerequisites in the international anarchy, domestic structure has little or no relevance to foreign policy. Such a conclusion ignores the role of a national government in a society and—perhaps more significantly—overlooks the important consequences of external relations on the internal development of political, economic, and social structures (Gourevitch, 1978).

With respect to decisions for war, power politics assumes that a national government and its population are separate entities: an autonomous political actor—the state—acts solely on its definition of the national interest. Similarly, the environmental perspective argues that a national interest is derived completely from society, taken as a multidimensional whole—thus denying the relevance of power politics. But an exclusive focus on social forces ignores the role of government in conducting foreign policy, because the ruling elites that dominate national government need not share values or preferences in common with the masses or other important interest groups.

Nonetheless, because decisions for war are based on the objectives and calculations of national governments that are more or less responsive to domestic pressures, the *variable* relationship of government to society is important. If power politics is taken as the essential basis of decisions for war, then domestic structure represents the internal environment for governmental action.

Potential constraints on decisions for war can emanate from many dimensions of the domestic structure. For example, it has long been argued that public opinion limits or at least complicates choice, while the transformation of domestic structures accompanying socioeconomic change provides more general insights on constraints. Key issues in state-society relationships can be examined in a dynamic framework. In addition, the changing composition of national governments as a result of socioeconomic change suggests that simple definitions of national interest and the calculation of the costs and benefits of war are no longer possible.

Public Opinion and War

Belief in the peaceful nature of democratic forms of government is based on faith in the goodness of ordinary citizens. According to Jeremy Bentham (1843), the "natural law" was not the selfish competition for personal gains at the expense of others but instead followed the principle of the "greatest happiness for the greatest number." From this utilitarian principle, John Stuart Mill argued that public opinion asserts a pacifying influence on government because peace is in the interest of the many, whereas war benefits only a few.[3] The spread of knowledge would thus make it possible for all members of the community to "reason rightly" and, by extension, to "act rightly" to avoid war. It was a common Enlightenment notion that public opinion, if allowed to make itself effective, would be sufficient to prevent war. War was a failure of

3. Mill's thoughts are best represented in his *Essay on Government*, Ernst Baker (ed.), (Cambridge: 1937). See also Carr (1939, pp. 22–26).

understanding, and reason could demonstrate the absurdity of power politics.

Furthermore, foreign policies had to be taken out of the hands of princes and kings and placed in the benign hands of the people, for whom war holds the prospect of greatest loss. Both Rousseau and Kant argued that, since wars were waged by princes and kings, there would be no wars under a republican form of government.[4] Citizens armed with the awareness of the costs of war would keep their nation at peace. Although peace is not the only ground upon which democratic institutions can be defended, this argument was implicitly or explicitly advanced by liberals of the nineteenth century.

The ideals of the Enlightenment thinkers and their liberal democratic followers were not borne out by the events and social movements of the nineteenth century. The power of reason over war did not seem to apply to the masses, who in the period after the French Revolution rallied to national causes in war and did not limit the propensity of governments to choose war; nationalism outweighed pacificism as the main current of public sentiment. Nevertheless, Woodrow Wilson attempted to revive faith in democracy and public opinion during the First World War, arguing that public opinion had a direct and pacifying influence on the actions of governments:

National purposes have fallen more and more into the background; and the common purpose of enlightened mankind has taken their place. The counsels of plain men have become on all hands more simple and straightforward and more unified than the counsels of sophisticated men of affairs, who still retain the impression that they are playing a game of power and are playing for high stakes. That is why I have said that this is a people's war, not a statesmen's. Statesmen must follow the clarified thought or be broken (1927, p. 259).

As with the Enlightenment writers, Wilson's words reflect normative concerns more than an accurate description of the sources of

4. The best treatment of Kant's and Rousseau's writings on the issue of war is in Waltz (1959, pp. 162–86).

foreign policy. But the ideal of the peaceful effect of democracy and public opinion was revived after a long decline.

The emergence of mass-based political systems as a pacifying influence on foreign policy remains questionable, however. E. H. Carr noted the increasing influence of public opinion but found its pacifying effects an idealistic supposition: "The nineteenth-century belief in public opinion comprised two articles: first (and in democracies this was with some reservations true), that public opinion is bound in the long run to prevail and second (this was the Benthamite view), that public opinion is always right" (1939, p. 31). In other words, public opinion alone is not a constraint on decisions for war.

Whatever the hopes of advocates for the role of public opinion, the analytic problem rests with the ability to chart how mass attitudes are translated into foreign policy. Unless public opinion guides foreign policy through a vague process of "osmosis," the institutional processes of the linkage between public opinion and foreign policy must be specified (Cohen, 1973).

In the end, one is left with an unsatisfying conclusion: public opinion, where it is allowed to express itself, has acquired a role in foreign policy, but it is uncertain whether this role constrains decisions for war. A broader framework is required. If domestic structure plays a role in decisions for war, then public opinion as a constraint on choice is part of a larger constellation of socioeconomic forces that shape relations between the state and society, defined as interrelationship of government and citizens. If power politics requires that a nation's foreign policy follow the logic of the external situation, especially the distribution of military capability, then a direct challenge to power politics is the observation that foreign policy must also match the domestic structure that generates it. By placing government in a domestic environment as well as in an international one, questions about the relevance of public opinion and constraints on decisions for war can be addressed.

Socioeconomic Change and State-Society Relationships

Even the simplest of models describing state-society relations helps organize the relationship of domestic structure to foreign policy. Power politics theories posit a "statist" model, wherein the interests of national government are detached from society and self-generated. For scholars of the power-politics school, a statist model allows for convenient assumptions about the national interest, even if it is defined as what the state perceives (Wight, 1946, p. 76). And since the security environment defines objectives, the origin of state interests is not a concern.

To examine a government's domestic environment, it is not necessary to formulate a complicated model of state-society relations (see Krasner, 1978, pp. 7–34; Nordlinger, 1981). Instead, the mere relaxation of assumptions of state autonomy permits a role for domestic structure in foreign policy. National governments thus exist as the central political authority in a nation, but they must continually interact with the many elements of society in order to generate the resources necessary to maintain the order that preserves their authority at home and resist threats from abroad. State power does not materialize out of thin air; governments must organize themselves to penetrate society and extract the resources necessary both to stay in office and ward off external threats (Tilly, 1975). The distinction between national government and its societal resource base is thus a sufficient, albeit limited, conceptual framework to explore domestic structure and war.

The domestic structure can also be viewed as dynamic. As Ernst Haas noted, power politics presumes the identification of national interest detached from socioeconomic change. The statist model is aptly labeled, because it describes both the sole actor in foreign policy of policy—the state—and also connotes the static nature of the state's interests. But the emergence of central-government authority represents an evolutionary transformation of domestic structure that does not end with the appearance of a strong state actor. Stein Rokkan's stages in the development of European societies illustrate the direction of change and the growing complication of state-society relations (1975). In the first period of "state formation" the central government is constructed. Three tasks must be accomplished in order to establish its authority over an otherwise chaotic or feudal social order: resources must be mobilized through taxation, an army must be organized to consolidate the territorial domain of the central government, and internal order must be established by police or the army. In the end, a unified elite with the resources to dominate other elements of society guides the central government.

A second period of "nation-building" obscures the delineation of state and society spheres essential to statist assumptions and the unencumbered execution of foreign policy. In this phase, contacts expand between the elite and larger sectors of population. These ties between government and population include the creation of conscript armies, provision of schooling, growth of mass media, regulation of commercial activity, or the provision of economic services; the autonomy of central government is thus replaced by a more complicated relationship characterized by societal demands and constraints on government. Rokkan identifies two additional stages in the development of Western European nations, but it is difficult to generalize beyond the European experience. A stage of greater participation, through the extension of civil and political rights and the formation of political parties, follows nation-building. Thereafter, societal goals lead to a last stage of redistribution of socioeconomic resources. The evolution of state-society relations thus works against the autonomy and restricted interests of the state.

Changing domestic structure falls under the broad rubric of modernization. Although an ambiguous concept, the process of modernization emphasizes the multidimensionality of social change (see Levy, 1966; Morse, 1976, pp. 1–21). If domestic structure is a constraint on decisions for war, the process of modernization must modify political institutions so as to alter the foreign policy of a government. For an otherwise unencumbered government, these new political institutions must limit or modify choices based on a self-generated definition of national interest.

In its most general sense, modernization describes how increasing (1) education, science, and technology, (2) organizational capacities, and (3) social mobilization leads to greater levels of industrialization, urbanization, and bureaucratization of society (Flora, 1981). These underlying growth processes lead to an expanding economy and population, which are accompanied by rising political participation and governmental intervention in society. But there is no one path of modernization. The concept as used here is intentionally ambiguous because underlying growth patterns are unique to each nation and the timing and pace of economic and population growth or the degree of political participation and government intervention vary enormously (see Migdal, 1983). Despite the inability to chart a common path of modernization, these changes have occurred in every nation of the world, although at different times and with different rates of change.

If modernization is used as a summary concept for socioeconomic change in society, the remaining question becomes how such changes alter the domestic structure of government and constrain its use of force against other governments. Two complementary approaches explain this linkage of socioeconomic change to government. On the one hand, the underlying growth processes of modernization enlarge the size and proportion of the population able to monitor and participate in government: greater political participation alters the *priorities* of government. On the other hand, the growing complexity of modernizing societies leads to greater governmental intervention in society: greater government intervention alters the *responsibilities* of government.

Analysis of the transformation of domestic structure through growing political participation follows the tradition of Max Weber (1947), who saw central government as the dominant actor, but one responsive to a changing society. From this perspective, modernization of domestic structure can be seen as the gradual emergence of a new system of governmental authority consisting of (1) a distributing elite that monopolizes policy-making, (2) service bureaucracies that administer policies, (3) social clienteles that generate demands on government (Flora and Heidenheimer, 1981, pp. 22–23). It is the proliferation of social clienteles—interest groups—that transforms domestic structure. The growth of political participation through interest groups dilutes distinct state interests because government assumes additional societal priorities.

These new demands alter the priorities of government (see Berger, 1981). Weber's conception of democratic capitalism describes how the demands for an open marketplace and economic efficiency transformed political institutions in the nineteenth century (Weber, 1947). In the case of the welfare state, increasing demands for socioeconomic equality or the institutionalization of social rights are translated into governmental priorities in relation to civil and political rights. The objectives of external strength and security are expanded to include internal economic freedom, equality before the law, and the provision of social services in a standard and routinized way (Flora and Heidenheimer, 1981). Ultimately, modernization creates new interest groups that establish new priorities for government, in response to which new political institutions are established and state-society relations are transformed.

The changing priorities of government are also accompanied by an altered basis of legitimacy, defined as the sources of tenure for the "distributing elite." As the priorities of government change, the performance of government officials is evaluated on a different basis. If priorities shift from external security (associated with the wealth of the state) to include the economic prosperity of key business groups or society as a whole, for example, then the rule of officials will be jeopardized in times of poor economic performance as well as of threat from abroad. The mechanisms of challenge to the tenure of governments vary widely across national political systems, but whether challenge comes from revolution or election, governments are held accountable for a larger and more complicated agenda.

For changing priorities of government to constrain decisions for war, and thus challenge the power-politics assumption of security-dominated national interest, socioeconomic change must be translated into the modernization of governmental structures that make foreign policy (Deutsch, 1961); modernization outside the institutions of government is not enough. Increasing political participation reflects a growth in the number of interest groups in a society demanding control of greater and more diverse services and resources of government; this in turn has a direct impact on the formal or institutional distribution of authority. In other words, influential interest groups are incorporated into the institutional machinery of government. The alternative is direct confrontation with the central government, a more revolutionary situation that often leads to the establishment of institutions that favor new action groups that dominate the former elites.

The link between interest groups and government leads to the consideration of configurations of political institutions. The development of legislatures and representative forms of government is the most obvious form of institutional arrangement for the "pluralist" articulation of interest demands in government. While there are many variations in the roles and authority of national legislatures, each constitutes an effort to translate political participation by the population into the machinery of government. Even when a government seeks to coopt or placate interest groups through their representation in powerless assemblies, it is a sign of detachment but also of awareness that growing desires for broader political participation must be met through new public programs.

Elections are the most direct translation of political participation into government. In the absence of electoral choice, however, voting itself does not represent the articulation of public concerns. The demands of multiple interest groups, as the agents of new priorities for government, can be expressed only in competitive electoral systems that allow for opposition political parties. As parties develop, greater portions of the population are enfranchised and governments become responsive to the public: "With due allowance for how tortuously and unevenly this transition occurred historically, logically the sequence can be reconstructed neatly. To put it sweepingly, a government responsible to the houses [legislatures] also becomes, in the long run, a government responsible to the people and thereby a *responsive* government, a government attentive to, and influenced by, the voice of the people" (Sartori, 1976, p. 20). Following Sartori's summary of the development of parties, an initial enfranchisement transforms a parliamentary party into an electoral (vote-seeking) party and leads to "responsive" government. Party government arises from party solidification and the development of a party system. Broad enfranchisement then creates mass parties that are outwardly-oriented and appeal to the demands of the public or specific interest groupings (Sartori, 1976, pp. 18–24). Whatever the institutional arrangements that structure party competition in elections and government, the end product is a government that responds to priorities established by an electorate. Autonomous state interests are challenged by a voting public and the political parties that attract their votes.

Government bureaucracy must also be responsive to domestic structure, even though the autonomy of state interests is more pronounced in the administrative structure of government. According to Weber, the bureaucratic elite is less vulnerable to outside interests and instead builds strong organizational interests. However, bureaucratic structures are unlikely to be completely isolated from socioeconomic change. If the distributing elite reflects competition among competing interest groups, bureaucracy can hardly avoid the external pressures, because "it is difficult to see how bureaucracy developed as a handmaiden to a system of representative government could be other than passive, dependent for initiatives on external forces, the onslaught of zealots, the pre-occupations of the experts and the periodic goads of the politicians worried about electoral survival" (Sutherland, 1972, p. 11). From the perspective of changing governmental priorities, modernization transforms domestic structure through the growth in the proportion and power of the population to participate in government. Autonomous government interests are circumscribed by interest groups, political parties, and national legislatures that share in setting the priorities for government. Elections permit social clienteles to influence a distributing elite directly. Finally, even bureaucracy becomes subject to the demands of interest groups able to participate in government. To the extent and degree that political participation is manifested in governmental priorities, national interest is no longer defined solely in terms of security. In addition, many avenues are opened to influence policy and decisions for war.

Another perspective on the modernization of domestic structure, in the tradition of Durkheim (1947), focuses on increasing economic specialization and the fragmentation of society (functional-structural differentiation). In other words, a more complicated division of production and consumption produces change in domestic structure. In particular, as specialization and fragmentation increase through socioeconomic change—industrialization, urbanization, and bureaucratization—institutions of government take over functions formerly performed by smaller social units, and the responsibilities of government expand. Increased government intervention in society is the result, and state-society distinctions become blurred by the complex mixture of responsibilities.

Whereas growing political participation alters the basis of governmental legitimacy, functional-structural differentiation transforms societal values. However, value change is difficult to trace. Ronald Inglehart (1977) argues that modernization, especially industrialization and economic prosperity, serves to satisfy the basic human needs of shelter, food, and personal security for an increasingly large portion of the population. This process, bound in social differentiation, changes values by increasing emphasis on an individual's needs for belonging, esteem, and self-realization. The consequences for domestic structure are as follows (Inglehart, pp. 4–18):

- Change in prevailing political issues; increasing salience of "life-style" issues
- Change in social bases of political conflict; relative decline in class conflict
- Changes in support for established national institutions; declining legitimacy of nation-state; rise of supranational and "tribal" or local loyalties
- Change in prevailing types of political participation; declining elite-directed political mobilization; rise of elite-challenging issue-oriented groups

Inglehart's model of value change incorporates the complementary role of political participation through increasing levels of social communication and its conduciveness to the rise of interest groups, but changing values produced by modernization are essential to the transformation of domestic structure.

The changing role of government can also be seen in the distribution of governmental resources. Over the past centuries, as a function of modernization and the accompanying increase in governmental responsibilities, the amount of wealth taxed and spent for social and economic services has expanded. The public-expenditure trends of advanced industrial societies since 1870 show that, in most countries, between one-third and one-half of gross national product is taxed and used for public programs (Kohl, 1983). Defense—the portion of spending that directly addresses security concerns—is rarely over 10 percent of GNP, and only in a few nations, notably the United States, is it greater than 20 percent of public spending. Defense has thus gone from a dominant expenditure item in the public-finance accounts of industrialized nations to one overshadowed by expenditure for social and economic services (OECD, 1978).

In the advanced industrial democracies, the structure of public spending is often characterized as the welfare state, wherein government assumes a measure of responsibility for meeting basic human needs through the provision of social services. Frederic Pryor (1968) has observed that similar expenditure patterns exist for industrialized centrally planned economies when viewed in a macroeconomic perspective. Although the operation of public services is different in the two systems, the structure of spending reflects a comparable set of responsibilities assumed by industrialized societies.

The expenditure priorities of non-industrialized nations displays the changing responsibilities of government produced by modernization. Using the World Bank's categorization of levels of economic development, the shift away from spending on defense can be documented as an aggregate trend (World Bank, 1983, table 26, pp. 198–99). In 1980, the governments of low-income economies (weighted by population) allocated 16.9 percent of central government expenditure to defense, middle-income economies 14.2 percent, and the governments of industrial market economies 12.5 percent.

Socioeconomic change thus produces governments that can no longer deal with security concerns in isolation from numerous other tasks. Given the limited resources available to government, choices must be made to allocate resources to meet many responsibilities; tradeoffs are possible and the primacy of security and the use of force may be constrained by the need to provide social services or enhance economic performance. Moreover, if societal values have evolved toward a reduced loyalty or support for the idea of the nation-state, then the pursuit of power politics is constrained by a society that will no longer sacrifice more valued social programs for security interests, especially if they involve the expense of war.

Changing government priorities and responsibilities are two sides of the same coin. As a constraint on war, however, the presence of institutional actors that limit choice seems more relevant

41

because broadening responsibilities need not curb security concerns and the use of force unless it can be shown that societal value change has occurred and has been translated into government. Accordingly, increased public participation and its transformation of institutional arrangements represents the most direct constraint on government.

Both perspectives on the transformation of domestic structure through modernization argue that state-society relations have undergone a profound alteration that makes it much more difficult to delineate clearly between state and society. Indeed, the concept of domestic structure encourages the exploration and modeling of the relationships between the many objectives of government and the diverse demands placed upon it by a population. Taken together, the growing priorities and responsibilities of government have altered domestic structure. Whether such changes constrain decision for war is an open question. Stanley Hoffmann has observed such a relationship in some political systems:

In democratically governed societies, there is going to be both pluralism and the predominance in the political sphere of those values which prevail in the social order. Moreover, in democratic political systems the main mode of political life is what Aron called "satisfaction quereleuse" or, as I prefer to put it, non-cataclysmic permanent dissatisfaction: the politics of universal bargaining. Now, the politics of universal bargaining and incremental compromise is very far indeed from the military virtues, and tends to erode or push down whatever basic consensus exists in the society. It is when the kind of values that I have mentioned coincide with a democratic political system that the decline of the acceptability of force is likely to be greatest (1973, p. 102).

The meaning of national interest, which is so vital to power politics, is clouded by the modernization of societies. The goal of security must compete with a large and crowded agenda of economic and social objectives. To the extent that other demands monopolize the agenda and resources of government, foreign policy based solely on the primacy of security is constrained.

The alteration of the domestic political structure of societies is a prominent feature of modernization, as it emphasizes the changing role of government and the changing composition of societies. But modernization has also provided opportunities for nations to develop different levels and kinds of interaction. In particular, industrialization leads to greater productive specialization and possibilities for international trade designed to take advantage of a greater global division of production. The growth of international commerce marks a most dramatic change in global relations, one that has generated many notions of transformation, not only in economic exchange, but also in social and political relations.

If modernization facilitates international commercial exchanges, then economic interests may grow to challenge government's preoccupation with security. The doctrine of free-trade liberalism first challenged the mercantilist and power politics orientation of pre-industrial governments (see Buzan, 1984) by asserting the generally pacifying influence of commercial relations, but foreign trade can take several paths to restrict decisions for war. To provide a constraint, foreign trade and the interest in protecting commercial enterprise must undermine the primacy of a government's security interests.

Classical Free-Trade Liberalism and Peace

Although many scholars and observers prefer to separate political and economic relations, economic reasoning has long been applied to the study of government and international politics, including the relationship between commerce and war (Silberner, 1946). Since early political economists challenged the domination of society and economy by a central government, the theme of commerce as an antidote to war was important to their arguments.

Adam Smith was the earliest popular advocate of the belief that increases in international trade would make war less profitable and therefore less likely. In some detail, he noted that the eighteenth-century mercantilist system emphasized accumulation of wealth by the government and the continual need to raise funds for war, which was thought to be the appropriate means to protect and acquire additional wealth, particularly precious metals (Smith, 1976, pp. 444–66). Under this system, taxes required to maintain a permanent military establishment negated any economic benefit of peace. In fact, domestic commerce dominated by a mercantilist government benefits from war because of increased demand and public expenditure for goods and services: "Translated into common language, mercantilist policy signified: prohibition, reprisals, export subsidies, prescription, continual commercial wars and meant armed conflicts. It led fatally to war because it meant a desire to impose on others obligations devoid of any reciprocity" (Silberner, quoted in Morse, 1976, p. 30).

From Adam Smith onward, prominent economic thinkers from competing schools of political economy generally agreed that war was inconsistent with economic progress. This consensus is not remarkable in itself, but it was a challenge to mercantilist doctrines that saw war as a necessary means to acquire wealth. Free-trade liberals like John Stuart Mill and John MacCulloch saw war as costly interference in commerce, and even protectionists like Frederic List viewed war as a blight on the development of national industrial economies. Finally, socialists like Karl Marx saw that war interrupted an otherwise inevitable evolution toward the classless society.

Many political economists, especially free-trade liberals, thought that new forms of economic organization would inhibit governments' choice for war. To some, unfettered international trade would melt away the need for war. The doctrine of free trade, embodied in the Manchester School, touted the virtues of commerce (Bullock and Shock, 1956); its most visible advocate was Richard Cobden: "I see in the Free-Trade principle that which shall act on the moral world as the principle of gravitation in the universe,— drawing men together, thrusting aside antagonism of race, and creed, and language, and uniting us in the bonds of eternal peace" (1870 vol. 1, pp 362).

John Stuart Mill saw the process of change in less dramatic, although equally panoramic terms:

Commerce first taught nations to see with good will the wealth and prosperity of one another. Before, the patriot, unless sufficiently advanced to feel the world his country, wished all countries weak, poor, and ill-governed, but his own; he now sees in their wealth and progress a direct source of wealth and progress to his own country. It is commerce which is rapidly rendering war obsolete, by strengthening and multiplying the personal interests which are in natural opposition to it. And it may be said without exaggeration that the great extent and rapid increase of international trade, in being the principal guarantee of the peace of the world, is the great permanent security for the uninterrupted progress of the ideas, the institutions, and the character of the human race (1909 book 3, p. 582).

The British were not alone in promoting the peaceful virtues of free trade; the Frenchman Frederic Bastiat, for example, made equivalent arguments: "Trade barriers constitute isolation, isolation gives rise to hatred, hatred to war, and war to invasion" (1922, p. 116). Throughout Western Europe, free-trade doctrine came to dominate economic reasoning as the industrial revolution led to rapid economic growth and a sharp increase in foreign trade.

With the expansion of private business and laissez-faire practices in the nineteenth century and their emphasis on the trade of primary and manufactured goods, the state withdrew from the goal of accumulation of wealth through taxation and conquest (Polanyi, 1944). The power of government was no longer dependent upon the possession of precious metal; instead, it derived its resources from the taxation of commercial interchange. Governments acquired a stake in industrialization and growth as a means to expand their sources of revenue, and business interests became powerful. Free-trade liberalism thus replaced mercantilism as the organizing principle of economic activity. Foreign trade restricted by the government, which frequently led to conflict, was replaced by an international environment conducive to the cooperative exchange of goods.

The alteration of the economic role of government represents a dramatic reorientation of international politics (Hinsley, 1963; Morse, 1976, pp. 50–59). Free-trade liberalism argues that the interest of government is served by the development of unrestricted patterns of free exchange based on mutual advantage and not by the protection of special advantages and spheres of influence. But government has in fact become more involved in regulation of the economy, and intervention to protect privileged positions or certain economic sectors has occasionally taken place. A protectionist school of economics arose to counter the arguments and influence of the free-traders, with a message that was straightforward and consistent with power politics: as long as nations continue to go to war, governments must protect their national economies as a way to extend national power. Although not influential in his lifetime, Frederic List was the most articulate advocate of protectionism, and protectionist notions became influential in Germany in the latter part of the nineteenth century (see Silberner, 1946 book 2, pp. 131–205).

Interestingly, Karl Marx, the most influential critic of free-trade capitalism, concurred with the liberal belief in the peaceful effects of free trade. The *Communist Manifesto* states that "national differences and antagonisms between peoples are vanishing gradually from day to day, owing to the development of the bourgeoisie, to freedom of commerce, to the world market, to uniformity in the mode of production and in the conditions of life corresponding thereto" (p. 29). Although Marx believed free trade to be an integral component of capitalism's exploitation of the working class, he viewed it as less harmful than protectionist policies.

As in the linkage of public opinion to decision for war, it is insufficient to assert that the existence of powerful commercial interests will constrain a government's use of force. Since force may otherwise be used to advance economic interests, a relationship between foreign-trading interests and government must be established that constrains decisions of war; economic interests must be translated into government policies that limit power politics.

Interdependence, Interpenetration, and Interconnection

Unlike domestic structure, foreign trade can pose an international or external constraint on decisions for war, as well as an internal one (Katzenstein, 1976). The external constraint is the increased vulnerability that comes from economic interdependence, which raises the costs of breaking profitable trading relations and directing resources away from commerce and toward war. The internal constraint stems from the interpenetration of nations by cosmopolitan trading interests. As a distinct and powerful interest group, foreign-traders challenge the definition of national interest as security alone. Taken together, the external and internal dimensions of foreign trade combine to limit the use of force through the greater interconnection of societies. As national economies become more sensitive to external developments and subject to the aspirations and demands of citizens, governments are forced to protect prosperity through cooperation with other governments.

The external restraint is the most obvious and is produced by the process of interdependence that is fostered by expanded commercial relations between economies. If not managed by government to preserve explicit goals of security—such as self-sufficiency or assured access to defense-related material—interdependence may result in vulnerability to the actions of others (Waltz, 1970). The economic costs of war, in such a situation, will outweigh security benefits.

This perspective on foreign trade challenges a key assumption in theories of international relations based on power politics, which assumes that the security interests defined by independent governments will dominate economic interests (Waltz, 1979). In the power-politics view, economic activity is a contributing element of the national resource base used to provide military capability. Further, the management of economic resources as a means to influence other governments and protect the national interest is a form of power politics. An autonomous economic interest does not exist, because the primacy of security rules out compromises between the pursuit of power and prosperity.

To assert that the interdependence and vulnerabilities resulting from trade influence the calculations of government is to argue that a national government cannot fully control or chooses not to regulate the interactions between its population and other nations. If a government could limit commercial activity to security-promoting exchange, decisions for war could not be constrained by the vulnerability of its economy to the actions of others. From the power-politics view, interdependence cannot alter a government's choice unless it is not in control of external economic ties. Governments unable to dominate economic interests challenge this assertion by demonstrating that state-society relations can favor the population—particularly private business interests—at the expense of the government's preoccupation with public security.

The domestic constraints posed by foreign trade are twofold and focus on the foreign-trading business community as a distinct interest group. First, heavy involvement in foreign trade increases the exposure of business elites to international communications and transaction; this exposure presumably produces more cosmopolitan outlooks, increased interpenetration of societies, and dilution of national identity. A second process is more obvious, given the earlier discussion of political participation: the larger the role for foreign traders in a national economy, the greater are their resources and power as a special interest group in society.

Robert Angell (1969) argues that international commerce will lead to more pacifistic outlooks. While offering no direct evidence, Angell posited that foreign travel and interaction with other foreign business elites would reduce loyalty to the sovereign state and replace it with new faith in transnational organization and institutions incapable of waging war.

Two studies of attitudes shed some light on the relative degree of dovishness of business elites engaged in foreign trade. In 1956, Daniel Lerner reported that in a sample of 757 French business leaders who were asked whether they supported the proposal for a European Defense Community (EDC) as opposed to the preservation of the French national army, those doing no export business supported the EDC by a ratio of two to one. Among those whose export business amounted to less than half of total volume, the ratio rose to three to one. For business elites for whom exports accounted for greater than half of their firm's volume, the ratio was six to one. If support for the EDC is seen as a transferal of loyalty away from the national government and its independent ability to wage war, then Angell's assertion of the pacifiying nature of international commerce is consistent with these findings.

A more recent study is more ambiguous about the relatively pacifistic nature of business elites. In a 1972 survey of U.S. military and business elites conducted by Bruce Russett and Elizabeth Hanson (1975), business elites in foreign-trading firms were contrasted with executives in non-trading firms. In a comparison of indices of relative hawkishness, elites in trading firms were not found to be significantly different in their values from non-trading executives, although both were much more dovish than military elites. The study did support the more general free-trade notion of business being more interested in peace, although the inclusion of a disproportionate number of defense-contracting firms, which have large foreign sales and executives with military orientations, if not career backgrounds, might have biased the findings.

The interconnection of nations is a third source of constraint on governments. As foreign trade grows with the process of industrialization, national economies become sensitive to the performance of other economies; economic performance at home is influenced from developments abroad (Cooper, 1968). If citizens demand prosperity, governments must act to satisfy domestic expectations through greater policy coordination with other governments.

Robert Keohane and Joseph Nye (1977) argue that the interconnection of nations produces complex interdependence, a situation wherein non-security interests dominate a government's foreign-policy agenda. Non-governmental actors, especially firms and international organizations, assume greater importance in international relations because their actions are likely to influence economic performance. As a result, force is less useful as an instrument of policy because it is unlikely to compel compliance over economic actors.

The basis of constraint on decisions for war is the transformation of government to serve economic as well as security interests (Morse, 1976). While the values and outlooks of international businessmen are difficult to determine, the effects of increased international trade on the conduct of diplomacy are apparent in the transformation of governments in response to new interests. The expansion of bureaucratic structures to fulfill a variety of domestic needs has already been noted, but some of this expansion was necessary to facilitate foreign trade (the U.S. Department of Commerce and European ministries of foreign trade are evidence of greater attention to the management of foreign commerce, while the Japanese ministry of international trade and industry is one of the most powerful agencies in the Japanese government). Since the 1960s, the United States has repeatedly reorganized agencies managing foreign trade in an era that witnessed an expansion of exports from a historical level of 5 percent to over 10 percent of GNP.

More telling in terms of security policy is the effect of greater commercial interaction on the traditional institutions of diplomatic statecraft. Before the First World War, the diplomatic corps of each foreign ministry was formally separate from the consular service, which attended to the commercial interests of the nation, and consular officials were often regarded as dealing with menial tasks. Although few studies examine the incorporation of business interests into contemporary diplomatic practices, a detailed study by Paul Lauren describes the situation prior to the First World War:

Prior to the twentieth century, Ministries of Foreign Affairs had relatively little involvement with commercial matters. Although cooperation between government officials and business interests had a long tradition, overseas transactions always remained within restricted bounds. In part, this was due to the limited amount of foreign trade, to philosophical assumptions regarding the value of laissez-faire, and to the inability of businessmen to sufficiently pressure their governments for more protection and assistance. This condition also resulted from the attitude among professional diplomats that their time should be spent on solving the vastly more "important" political problems rather than the mundane questions of "inferior" commercial matters. As a result, foreign ministries created administrative structures that reinforced these prejudices, assumed few responsibilities for commercial matters, employed staffs inexperienced with graphs or figures, and maintained little contact with the business world. In the words of one diplomat: "The great flaw in the system was that economics had no place in it; the subject slightly alarmed a world still struggling against a predominance of prose" (1976, p. 154).

In the period between the two world wars, foreign ministries around the world corrected this imbalance, and large economic bureaus now figure prominently in the activities of professional diplomats.

Although free-trade liberals have long argued that foreign trade exerts a pacifying influence on governments, there must be mechanisms by which commercial interests are translated into a constraint on decisions for war. Interdependence limits governments by raising the economic costs of war beyond a tolerable level. If governments do not act to direct economic exchange toward security objectives, then a deep involvement in foreign trade will limit the use of force. Interpenetration transforms domestic structure to promote private economic interests at the expense of national government's concern for security. War is less likely to occur because governments are less able to define national interest in security terms. Finally, interconnection constrains decisions for war insofar as governmental institutions are transformed to satisfy public expectations for prosperity through the management of foreign-trading relations.

INTERNATIONAL ORGANIZATION AND PEACE

A government's choice to employ an international organization in its dealings with other governments may or may not signify the abandonment of power politics. If security concerns are not involved, collaboration in a multilateral forum may simply represent a more efficient way to manage relations. However, international organizations frequently deal with security issues, and their contribution to the peaceful resolution of disputes directly challenges the role of power politics in foreign policy. A government that chooses to abide by or appeal to principles supported by an international organization rejects the exclusivity of its own national interest. In short, a reliance on international organization is a governmental choice that precludes power politics.

The choice between power politics and international organization has been noted since the beginning of the European state system (see Jacobson, 1979, chap. 2). From a more narrow legal tradition,

Grotius ([1646] 1925) argued that a code of law could govern the conduct of relations between nations. Power politics asserts that the national interest overrides any notion of a just use of force. A system of law could provide normative standards to proscribe the use of force and restrain the ability of governments to use force without regard to a principle of justice. Although the ideals of Grotius and his followers had little if any effect on the practice of contemporary governments, advocates of international law saw that alternatives to power politics existed and attacked the ability of governments to define national interests on their own.

International law has since developed into an extensive and elaborate code but has not replaced national interest. Many theoreticians—including Rousseau, Bentham, and Kant—felt that power politics and the use of force could be restrained only through the construction of collaborative institutions that would support common values at the expense of national interest. If a community of governments could agree on common interests, the benefits of collaboration would challenge the need to define a national interest and use force to pursue it. For the European draftsmen of these peace plans, the common interest in the advancement of Christianity, the defense of Europe from the Turks, or the protection of ruling dynasties could replace the self-interest of national governments (see Hemleben, 1943).

A prominent early advocate of peace through international organization was Jean-Jacques Rousseau, who applied his notions of a social contract to international anarchy. Just as government was necessary to provide order to civil society, so must a federation of governments provide order to Europe:

The Federation must embrace all the important powers in its membership; it must have a Legislative Body, with powers to pass laws and ordinances binding upon all its members; it must have a coercive force capable of compelling every state to obey its common resolves whether in the way of command or prohibition; finally, it must be strong and firm enough to make it impossible for any member to withdraw at its own pleasure the moment he conceives his private interest to clash with that of the whole body (1917, pp. 59–60).

Supporters of Rousseau would agree that only a powerful world government able to enforce a rule of law can dominate the self-interests of governments and their use of force. Even scholars of the power-politics tradition recognize world government as the only potential alternative to international anarchy and its violent manifestations (Morgenthau, 1948 pp. 479–80). However, power politics itself precludes the movement toward world government.

The suppression of national interest through a federation of governments rests on a theory of collective goods and how it might be applied to relations among governments (Olson, 1968; Riker, 1964). If national governments can agree that the benefits derived from international collaboration are greater than the costs of pursuing national interest, then bargains can be struck among governments to form institutions to support common benefits at lower costs to the members of a federation (Keohane, 1984). With respect to security interests, if national security can be protected by a federation of governments, then the resort to power politics and self-help will be unnecessary.

Of course, the translation of these notions into the collective-security experiments of the League of Nations and the United Nations has not produced a record that supports the hypothesis that power politics has been restrained. Still, these efforts do represent examples of governments seeking to identify and advance principles of conduct that transcend national interest and power politics. The fact that the use of force persists indicates that the mechanisms of collective security were weak, not necessarily that organizations are unable to transcend power politics. From a collective-goods perspective, the benefits of collective security have not outweighed the benefits from pursuing national interest.

The inability of governments to agree on effective forms of federation and the collective pursuit of common interests suggests that a more suitable approach is to reduce the importance of national government through greater activity by international organizations. Since independent national governments are an essential requirement to power politics, the diminution of their role in international relations would limit the tendency to use force. Since governments cannot agree on common interests and federation, other agents of international interaction may become more important in developing common interests at the expense of power politics. This is the theory of functionalism, which observes that greater portions of international interaction are managed outside traditional diplomatic methods and at the expense of a government's ability to define and pursue a single national interest (Mitrany, 1966).

A panoramic perspective on functionalism sees national government as only one stage in the evolution of larger and more stable units for the governance of humanity (Rittberger, 1973). In this view, the value and importance of family units gave way to tribes, city-states, and then nations; international organizations are thus only the next stage in the development toward a global political unit. Whereas federalism constitutes a frontal assault on the independence of national governments and their use of force, functionalism is a process by which the independence of governments is circumscribed by greater and more intensive cooperation in fields in which the pressures toward collaboration are almost irresistible. Instead of expecting collaboration on the difficult issues of security and the independent authority of governments, cooperation on cultural and economic relations—which can be seen as the underlying material causes of conflict—can overwhelm power politics in the long run.

Limited and specific-purpose international organizations advance peace to the degree that they erode the scope and range of governmental authority in dealing with other nations: "Every activity organized in that way would be a layer of peaceful life, and a sufficient addition of them would create increasingly wide strata of peace—not the forbidding peace of an alliance, but one that would suffuse the world with a fertile mingling of common endeavor and achievement" (Mitrany, 1966, p. 70). Through the management of international organizations, the accumulation of material benefits to society, referring again to the collective-goods argument, will outweigh the benefits of preserving independent national government and the use of force.

A neo-functionalist variant of this process toward peace views governments as having to guide functional cooperation actively (Haas, 1958; Lindberg and Scheingold, 1970, pp. 6–11). In particular, politically important activities must be integrated into collaborative institutions. If power politics is to be replaced, governments must bargain to create political institutions and policies that can undermine the independence of governments so that the sectoral integration of governments will grow at the expense of the discrete interests of national government.

In the end, international organization serves to undermine power politics through the replacement of self-interest and rivalry with institutional arrangements to support common interests. From a collective-goods approach, the benefits of permanent collaborative arrangements outweigh the costs of the independent diplomacy associated with power politics. From a functionalist perspective, international organization reflects the decline of nationalism and the role of independent national governments in international relations. Finally, neo-functionalism describes the trend toward the collaborative management of international relations by governments. From each perspective, international organization serves to foster cooperative relations between governments based on whatever common interests exist. Since power politics and decisions for war rest on the pursuit of self-interest, participation in international organization poses a direct challenge to the use of force.

CHANGE AND WAR: THE RESULT FOR THEORY

As long as wars occur, we must recognize the persistent relevance of power politics. Violent force is a feature of world politics that calls attention to survival and security. In a decision for war, a government will identify the objectives of action, calculate the chance of success and, if forceful means match the ends, choose the use of force as an instrument of policy. These are the constant elements of war that cannot be ignored. In addition, these enduring features of a decision for war have profitably served to build theories of world politics based on the pursuit and distribution of power.

For theory to advance, however, the unchanging elements of war must be better understood as part of the ever-changing global system. In particular, more adequate theory must be able to deal with the direction and pace of socioeconomic change. Although the innumerable transformations in the global system might not have permeated the durable realities of power politics, it seems much more likely that change has shaped and constrained the basis of choice by governments. We know this to be true in all other aspects of governmental policy, and it should be no less true of foreign policy.

To accommodate both power politics and socioeconomic change requires a theoretical framework that accepts the elements of decisions for war but places them in the context of change. In the first instance, it is necessary to understand the changing bases of dispute between governments. This is an extremely complicated task, since the potential sources of conflict have expanded with the growing intensity and scope of interaction between societies. It is equally likely, however, that the nature of disputes that are prone to induce the use of force is constant. Although conflictual interactions may proliferate, issues that governments consider suitable to resolution or settlement by force remain the same. Governments will use force to expand territory, resolve contested boundaries and claims, or depose rival governments; they will not use force to settle other kinds of disputes—for example, to eliminate foreign-trade barriers, stop transnational environmental pollution, or control the flow of unwanted migration or refugees.

The most important theoretical contribution of power politics is calculating the prospect of successful use of force. In this element of war, governments believe, with a certain measure of uncertainty, that the application of force will resolve the objective in dispute. A means-ends test is a necessary component of any theory of war and fully consistent with the enduring presence of power politics.

The third element of war, that of governmental choice, is the focus of this book. Given a dispute prone to war and the belief that force can succeed, the decision by government to fight a war to obtain its objectives must be studied as part of a balance of inducements and constraints. Power politics provides the inducement: to use force successfully is to demonstrate the power of the national government in the global system. To use force is to protect or extend the "national interest," or more directly to enhance the security of the government. To compel one's will on another is the unambiguous manifestation of power politics, and the success of force as an instrument is the most tangible display of power.

While the inducements may remain constant, the constraints on decision for war will evolve and affect each government to variable degrees. There can be any number of constraints on decisions for war, some unique to a particular government. The configuration of inducements and constraints is specific to each decision for war, but focus on domestic structure, foreign trade, and international organization stems from the recognizable limitations of power politics itself. The actors in world politics are not all the same, they are representative of quite different domestic political structures that contain variable obstacles to governmental choice. The interests of government can vary, and the potential impact of foreign-trading interests may constrain decisions for war. Finally, force is not the only avenue to resolve disputes, and the alternative of conducting interactions through international organization may erode the value of force as an instrument of policy.

For war to occur, the inducements to decisions for war must overcome political constraints. This book investigates the potential constraints posed by domestic political structure, foreign-trading interests, and the commitment to international organizations. Above all, it is the changing development of constraints that is important. Over time, we should expect these constraints to have greater impact individually and taken as an interactive combination of determining factors.

3

DECISIONS FOR WAR

In this study, *decisions* that result in a policy of war on the part of national governments are the relevant behavioral phenomena of interest. Following the theoretical framework developed in chapter 1, which relates the element of choice to its environmental context, decisions for war can be compared in order to ascertain which factors may or may not systematically act to constrain the use of force. Before investigating specific hypotheses, however, it is necessary first to define decisions for war in a manner that delineates a particular class of behavior and, second, to outline a research strategy that will lead to analytically valid conclusions.

At the outset, it is necessary to distinguish war from other incidents of violence in world affairs. A number of available policy options employ some level or type of force less drastic than war, including threats, blockades, seizures, and punitive bombing raids (see, for example, Blechman and Kaplan, 1978; and Craig and George, 1983, part 2). Decisions for war are distinguished from these other uses of force by the commitment of substantial national resources to violent and sustained international conflict. The violence of the policy and its continuation are the identifying characteristics of war, features of policy not shared by any other more limited use of force. Decisions for war can be easily separated from all other decisions of government by observing their direct consequences: at least two independent national governments decide to commit human and material resources and lives to a policy designed to force capitulation or concession on the part of the other government. At least two governments must decide for war; otherwise an unreciprocated policy of war will produce capitulation and the avoidance of sustained violence. For example, the three Baltic nations yielded to annexation by the Soviet Union in 1939, yet later in that year Finland decided to make war rather than cede territory; similarly the Hungarian government resisted Soviet invasion in 1956, but the Czech government did not in 1968.

In this study, as in many others, the sustained use of violent force is called interstate war and operationally defined as a conflict that inflicted greater than one thousand battle-related deaths in the course of one year. By this definition, sixty-one such wars can be identified as having occurred since 1815.[1] One thousand battle deaths is an appropriate threshold for identifying *sustained* violence, because most wars far surpass that level. The sixty-one wars include some borderline cases, however, because available information is uncertain. The inclusion of these wars extends the range of comparison, and findings can be contrasted with more certain wars.[2] With few exceptions, the use of force either results in less than a few hundred battle deaths or erupts into war resulting in a far greater number of deaths. More importantly, incidents with less than one thousand deaths do not represent the sustained commitment of resources involved in the conduct of interstate war. Such uses of force are separate phenomena not directly related to the questions posed here.

Although at least one national government must initiate hostilities by being the first to decide for the sustained use of force, the

1. The population of instances of decisions for war used in this study is taken from Singer and Small, *The Wages of War* (1972). Although there are other studies using somewhat different criteria, notably Wright (1942) and Richardson (1960), Singer and Small's war list is based on explicit inclusion criteria and review of historical sources. Accordingly, the *Wages of War* has become the standard reference list of wars for use by scholars. The list has been somewhat modified and extended in Small and Singer, *Resort to Arms* (1982); some of these changes are incorporated into the population of decisions for war used here. Amendments to the Singer and Small (1972) list are discussed below. Wars occurring after 1965 are taken from reporting in *Strategic Survey*, an annual publication of the International Institute of Strategic Studies (London).

2. In the absence of definitive information, Small and Singer (1982) estimate the following wars at one thousand battle-related deaths; they qualify as borderline inclusions: Franco-Spanish (1823), Italo-Roman (1860), Italo-Sicilian (1860), Ecuador-Colombian (1863), Spanish-Chilean (1865), and three Central American wars (1885, 1906, and 1907). In addition, the 1982 Falklands War seems to barely surpass the one thousand battle-death threshold. Whatever the extent of casualties, each of these wars meet the requirement of governmental choice to use sustained and violent force.

analyses presented here do not distinguish between the initiating (or aggressor) and the responding (or victim) governments. Differentiating between which government first decided on war and which is responding to another's actions is difficult and its meaning ambiguous, since it need not be indicative of an "aggressive" government or one more anxious or more willing to use force. An example of the complexity of this issue is the onset of the Franco-Prussian War in 1870, in which France was the first to declare war, yet the Prussian government of Chancellor Bismarck is generally considered to have been the belligerent party (Howard, 1961). The outbreak of the First World War represents an even more ambiguous set of decisions for war, and scholars differ widely on assigning roles in the escalation to war (see Geiss, 1967, pp. 17–53). Except for wars of conquest (see chapter 4), the tit-for-tat diplomatic interaction and maneuvers prior to the outbreak of war are usually too complex to identify clearly which government first decides on war. However, an unambiguous case of aggression, such as the German invasion of Poland in 1939, can provide additional insights into the relevant inducements and restraints for decision-making.

Another important distinction is between governments deciding to start a war and those deciding to enter an ongoing war. National governments that first decide to use sustained and violent force are acting on the basis of the conflict of interest or specific issue that brought them to that outcome. Following the theoretical arguments presented in chapter 1, they resort to force in order to achieve particular objectives in dispute, and war is the instrument of policy. National governments deciding to join existing wars, on the other hand, are not entering war in response to particular disputed issues that brought about the original war. Instead, they decide to join based on the conduct and outcome of the ongoing war (Altfeld and Bueno de Mesquita, 1979). In short, their choice is contingent on the progress and implications of an existing war, and not necessarily on the original dispute. Their objective interest is to enter an ongoing war in order to gain territory or to influence or protect a valued position that has become threatened by the success of one belligerent.

In the analyses conducted here, national governments that decide for war more than one month after its onset are considered joining belligerents. Presumably, if the issue that brought nations to war was sufficiently salient to a national government to require force, then it would opt to use force within at least the first month of conflict (Small and Singer, 1982). Otherwise, other factors—especially the anticipated outcome of the ongoing war—encourage later entry into war. These other factors make decisions to enter an ongoing war substantively different from decisions to participate in the start of a war, and they are therefore excluded from the analyses conducted here. One month may be a somewhat long time period, but a particular and perhaps more reliable definition of original and joining belligerents would be impossible without careful study of each national decision for war to ascertain whether objectives in war match the dispute that began the war. An alternative is to restrict the analyses to only the first two governments to engage in war, but this is far too restrictive, especially when the participation of other governments is instrumental to the prolongation of violence beyond the threshold of one thousand battle deaths. For the purposes of this study, one month is an appropriate dividing line because no national government coded as a "joiner" decided to enter an existing war within two months of that cutoff (three months from the start of war).

Given these distinctions, it is possible to identify 217 national decisions for war in sixty-one interstate wars occurring from 1815 to 1986, forty-seven of which represent decisions to join an existing conflict (see table 3.1)

Two of the wars included in the Singer and Small list (1972) are excluded from the population of cases in table 3.1. The first, the battle of Navarino Bay in 1827, is omitted because it did not represent a decision on the part of any government to commit resources to a sustained use of force. Although the governments of Britain, France, and Russia had ordered a blockade of the Turkish fleet, the battle is generally considered a command failure and lasted one day (this war was dropped by Small and Singer [1982]).

A second exclusion is more complicated. Once a nation is at war, additional governments with which it wages war should be considered joining belligerents and not participants in a separate war. In other words, no nation can fight two completely separate interstate wars at once; it is either at war or not at war. For this reason, the

TABLE 3.1   INTERSTATE WARS AND PARTICIPANTS, 1815–1986

War	Year Begun	Original Belligerents	Joining Belligerents*
1. Franco-Spanish	1823	France Spain	
2. Russo-Turkish	1828	Russia Turkey	
3. Mexican-American	1846	Mexico United States	
4. Austro-Piedmont	1848	Austria Piedmont	
5. First Schleswig-Holstein	1848	Denmark Prussia	
6. Roman Republic	1849	Austria France Papal States Two Sicilies	
7. La Plata	1851	Argentina Brazil	
8. Crimean	1853	Russia Turkey	France (5) Britain (5) Piedmont (14)
9. Anglo-Persian	1856	Britain Persia	
10. Italian	1859	Austria France Piedmont	
11. Spanish-Moroccan	1859	Morocco Spain	
12. Italo-Roman	1860	Papal States Piedmont	
13. Italo-Sicilian	1860	Piedmont Two Sicilies	
14. Franco-Mexican	1863	France Mexico	
15. Ecuador-Columbian	1863	Ecuador Colombia	
16. Second Schleswig-Holstein	1864	Austria Denmark Prussia	
17. Lopez War	1864	Brazil Paraguay	Argentina (4)
18. Spanish-Chilean	1865	Chile Spain	Peru (3)
19. Seven Weeks	1866	Austria Baden	

*Figures in parentheses indicate the number of months after the onset of war at which belligerents joined.

Table 3.1 *Continued*

War	Year Begun	Original Belligerents	Joining Belligerents*
		Bavaria	
		Hanover	
		Hesse-Darm-stadt	
		Hesse-Kassel	
		Italy	
		Mecklenburg	
		Prussia	
		Saxony	
		Württemberg	
20. Franco-Prussian	1870	Baden	
		Bavaria	
		France	
		Prussia	
		Württemberg	
21. Russo-Turkish	1877	Russia	
		Turkey	
22. Pacific	1879	Bolivia	Peru (2)
		Chile	
23. Sino-French	1884	China	
		France	
24. Central American	1885	El Salvador	
		Guatemala	
25. Sino-Japanese	1894	China	
		Japan	
26. Greco-Turkish	1897	Greece	
		Turkey	
27. Spanish-American	1898	Spain	
		United States	
28. Russo-Japanese	1904	Japan	
		Russia	
29. Central American	1906	El Salvador	
		Guatemala	
		Honduras	
30. Central American	1907	El Salvador	
		Honduras	
		Nicaragua	
31. Spanish-Moroccan	1909	Morocco	
		Spain	
32. Italo-Turkish	1911	Italy	
		Turkey	

*Figures in parentheses indicate the number of months after the onset of war at which belligerents joined.

Continued on next page

Table 3.1 *Continued*

War	Year Begun	Original Belligerents	Joining Belligerents*
33. First Balkan	1912	Bulgaria Greece Serbia Turkey	
34. Second Balkan	1913	Bulgaria Greece Romania Serbia Turkey	
35. World War I	1914	Austria- Hungary Belgium France Germany Great Britain Japan Russia Serbia	Turkey (3) Italy (9) Bulgaria (14) Portugal (18) Romania (24) United States (32) Greece (34)
36. Hungarian-Allies	1919	Czechoslovakia Hungary Romania	
37. Greco-Turkish	1919	Greece Turkey	
38. Soviet-Polish	1920	Poland Soviet Union	
39. Manchurian	1931	China Japan	
40. Chaco	1932	Bolivia Paraguay	
41. Italo-Ethiopian	1935	Ethiopia Italy	
42. Sino-Japanese	1937	China Japan	Soviet Union (13) Mongolia (22) United States (53)
43. World War II	1939	Australia Canada France Germany New Zealand Poland South Africa Soviet Union	Norway (7) Belgium (8) Netherlands (8) Italy (9) Greece (14) Ethiopia (17) Yugoslavia (20) Romania (23) Finland (23)

*Figures in parentheses indicate the number of months after the onset of war at which belligerents joined.

Table 3.1   *Continued*

War	Year Begun	Original Belligerents	Joining Belligerents*
		United Kingdom	Hungary (23) Bulgaria (28) United States (28) Brazil (58)
44. Russo-Finnish	1939	Finland Soviet Union	
45. Palestine	1948	Egypt Iraq Israel Jordan Lebanon Syria	
46. Korean	1950	North Korea South Korea United States	United Kingdom (2) Philippines (3) Turkey (4) P.R. China (4) Australia (6) Canada (6) France (6) Belgium (7) Netherlands (7) Greece (7) Thailand (7) Ethiopia (10)
47. Russo-Hungarian	1956	Hungary Soviet Union	
48. Sinai	1956	Egypt France Israel United Kingdom	
49. Sino-Indian	1962	India P.R. China	
50. Kashmir	1965	India Pakistan	
51. Indochina	1965	North Vietnam South Vietnam United States	Australia (5) South Korea (15) Philippines (20) Thailand (32) Cambodia (61)

*Figures in parentheses indicate the number of months after the onset of war at which belligerents joined.

Continued on next page

Table 3.1 *Continued*

War	Year Begun	Original Belligerents	Joining Belligerents*
52. Six Day	1967	Egypt Israel Jordan Syria	
53. Football	1969	El Salvador Honduras	
54. Indo-Pakistani	1971	India Pakistan	
55. Yom Kippur	1973	Egypt Israel Syria	
56. Cyprus	1974	Cyprus Turkey	
57. Ogaden	1977	Ethiopia Somalia	
58. Cambodian-Vietnamese	1978	Cambodia Vietnam	P.R. China (17)
59. Ugandan-Tanzania	1978	Tanzania Uganda	
60. Persian Gulf	1980	Iran Iraq	
61. Falklands	1982	Argentina United Kingdom	

*Figures in parentheses indicate the number of months after the onset of war at which belligerents joined.

Russo-Japanese War of 1939 cannot be considered a separate war. Instead, considering the Soviet involvement in China at the time and Japanese ambitions in the Far East, it was an expansion of the Sino-Japanese War that began in 1937 (Ulam, 1968, pp. 249–50). Similarly, U.S. entry into World War II is included as an expansion of the Sino-Japanese War, since the Japanese initiation of hostilities in 1941 was directly connected to the ongoing war in China. Once the governments already waging war in Europe and North Africa were drawn into this Far Eastern war, the distinction between the two conflicts became meaningless. When the United States and United Kingdom with their allies became involved in both of the ongoing wars, the two wars can be considered one.

Two wars have been added to this list, in addition to those beginning since 1970. The 1864 war between Paraguay and Brazil was added despite uncertainty about Paraguay's population. The Soviet-Polish War which began in 1920 was excluded from the Singer and Small list (1972) because the Soviet government lacked the necessary number of diplomatic recognitions qualifying it for system membership until 1922. Small and Singer included these two wars and added six others before 1965 (1982, p. 58). I exclude the Boxer Rebellion (1900) and a Sino-Soviet war in 1929 because of the uncertain participation of the Chinese government. Three wars on the Small and Singer list should be classified as war expansion: Soviet-Japanese wars in 1938 and 1939 and the Franco-Thai War (1940). The Israeli-Egyptian War of Attrition (1969–70) is included by Small and Singer but does not represent a decision to apply sustained violent force, only intermittent retaliations. As for the wars since 1965, I differ from Small and Singer and categorize China's war with Vietnam as expansion of the ongoing war in Cambodia. I also exclude Afghanistan because an Afghani government did not decide to resist Soviet intervention. Finally, I add the 1982 Falklands War because it most clearly crossed the one thousand battle-death threshold and meets the requirements of governmental choice for war.

RESEARCH DESIGN

With these conceptual definitions of decisions for war and the identification of a population of such decisions, it is possible to turn to issues of research design. Given the theoretical interests of this study, two approaches are possible, one more appropriate than the other.

One possible approach, given the explicit focus on decisions, is to analyze discrete decision-making procedures that generate policy outcomes resulting in war (see the discussion in Snyder and Diesing, 1977). But to be useful, an accurate model of foreign-policy decision-making would be necessary in order to assess the relationship of the three trends of interest and decisions for war. Such a study is not currently feasible given the absence of (1) sufficient cross-national theoretical knowledge concerning foreign-policy decision-making, and (2) the absence of a sufficient body of data on decisions for war with which to validate any notions of the relationship of various factors. Although theory and data on foreign-policy decision-making are abundant, they are well developed for only a few governments and not readily generalizable. In addition, although some decisions for war have been examined in great detail, on most the information available is only sketchy and uneven. Until theory and data on decision-making have been developed, any studies based on the discrete analysis of decisions themselves would be subject to countless challenges to their validity.

However, it is possible to assess the importance of constraints on decisions for war and how they may operate to condition choice and delimit the opportunities to employ force. Quantitative indicators of constraints can be contrasted between governments going to war as opposed to those remaining at peace. One can only claim that a certain factor is related to decisions for war if national governments going to war can be observed to possess more or less of that attribute than governments that *do not* go to war. The general form of the hypothesis is, then: at the time of any war onset, the nations identified as initiating belligerents are significantly different according to a particular attribute from those that refrain from going to war.

The particular hypotheses, based on the theoretical discussions in chapter 2 on the three trends of interest to this study, can be generally stated as follows:

1. The greater the degree of domestic political openness and competition, the less likely a national government is to decide for war.
2. The greater the amount of international trade of a national economy, the less likely its national government is to decide for war.
3. The greater a national government's participation in international intergovernmental organizations, the less likely it will decide for war.

The confirmation or disconfirmation of these hypotheses is possible only if for each instance of decision for war, *all* the independent national governments in the global system are compared according to the relevant indicators. If the hypotheses as stated are to be confirmed, then governments going to war will have significantly less of a particular attribute than those that do not decide for war. These hypotheses, stated generally, can of course be further qualified by analyzing several specific indicators of each trend. For example, in investigating the relationship of domestic political structure and decisions for war, separate analyses can be conducted for limits on executive authority and political competition in order to investigate differences in their effect on any relationships.

The research that follows consists of cross-sectional analyses of the independent national governments in the global system during each year that war occurs. In this way, valid statistical inferences can be drawn based on the relative degree of constraint on each government in a year that war occurs. A conclusion that governments deciding for war are constrained by involvement in foreign trade, for example, is only valid when *all* governments are contrasted. Otherwise, the distinct characteristics of governments going to war cannot be separated from attributes that bear no relation to war participation. If, in a given year, nations going to war have little trade involvement, one can conclude that such an attribute is related to decisions for war only if the nations trade significantly less than others.

The uniqueness of this aspect of the research design cannot be overemphasized. One hundred and seventy decisions for war, the population of such behaviors since 1815, are studied individually. However, the choice for war is contrasted against the choice for peace by other governments. Although this is an onerous data requirement, a disaggregated analysis is the only suitable way to investigate decisions made by national governments.

The relationships found in these separate analyses can then be compared over time in order to investigate changing relationships and the determinants of decisions for war. Of particular interest are the changing relationships apparent during different historical diplomatic epochs. Major wars, such as the Napoleonic Wars, the wars of 1848, and the First and Second World Wars, have tended to introduce the greatest amount of change into the global system. As a result, various historical epochs can be delineated and the particular characteristics of these periods can be examined in relation to change.

Limitations and Conclusions

Before proceeding to the analysis of the hypothesized relationships, the limitations of the research design should be explicitly noted. Although change and transformations of the global system are being contrasted with more traditional power-politics notions expressing the constancy of factors determining decisions for war, these power-politics factors are not fully explicated or measured. This study examines the environmental constraints on governmental decisions for war. The motivations and calculations of the probability of success in war are critical elements in decisions for war, but they are not directly incorporated into these analyses. As explained in chapter 1, it is assumed—or more properly, posited—that the acceptability of the use of force in foreign policy, and by extension the willingness to wage war, is part of the traditional concept of international politics that underpins power politics. It is a logical necessity that key elites of independent national governments that go to war possess this willingness to use force and wage war as a national policy. This research hopes to establish the degree to which non-power-politics change in the global system can be seen to constrain this willingness to go to war over time.

The analyses in this study can shed light on the parameters of foreign-policy decision-making. The findings can be considered useful if one of two conclusions can be drawn. First, the understanding of war would be enhanced even if no relationship can be found between these three trends and decisions for war, and future research can be guided by the fact that a certain set of theoretical propositions can be excluded from consideration. This is not a critical test of the relevance of power politics. Nor does the absence of meaningful relationships suggest that there are not important limitations on the use of force. Nonetheless, if constraints on decisions for war do not emerge, then further investigations should focus on the durable nature of power politics and how it may have been modified over time.

If, on the other hand, the analyses conducted here discern reliable relationships between likely constraints and war, however qualified, then future studies of decisions for war should either incorporate these factors into analyses or account for them by substituting mediating variables. What is more likely in this instance is that additional analyses will be necessary to more completely elucidate the effect of changing global phenomena on decisions for war.

Several other caveats should be briefly mentioned. Only one form of the use of force is addressed: the most extreme application of force through war. Other levels of violence are not accounted for, and this leads to interesting questions for further research. In particular, have changes in the global system led to the substitution of other, perhaps more covert, means of coercion or force? Such a question serves to underline the wider context of conflict in which these analyses can be framed.

Finally, the change and constraints central to this research are largely derivative of the process of industrialization, which occurred first in Europe and North America, and only somewhat later in Japan. Can the questions posed here be considered Eurocentric? This is clearly not the case, since the analyses take into account that differential rates of industrialization have produced various effects in the global system. The hypotheses offered here are, of course, not formulated with only industrialized nations in mind, but it is important to examine the relationships of global trends to the occurrence of war in a global system that has experienced an increasing amount of stratification according to the wealth and industrialization of nations. Such considerations are important given an explicit interest in change.

4

DOMESTIC POLITICAL
STRUCTURE AND
DECISIONS FOR WAR

Thus far, the relationship between decisions for war and trends in the global system has been discussed only in general terms. Below, I specify more fully the relationship between domestic political structure and war, present indicators of relevant aspects of domestic structure, and proceed to explore empirical relationships between these indicators and decisions for war.

As shown in chapter 2, a strong case can be made that domestic structure influences decisions for war. Competitive political participation, in particular, acts as a constraint on the independent action of national political elites charged with the conduct of a government's foreign policy. As long as foreign policy is developed in the same political arenas in which leadership is contested and policies are formulated and executed, domestic structure cannot be separated from foreign policy. Thus, on the policy agenda of any national government for which political competition is permitted and political authority is shared, security issues are contested by rival political elites for the attention and resources of society. A decision to wage war—an extreme action that affects all other issues of governmental policy—requires the support of those responsible for other policies in order to assemble the necessary consensus to free sufficient resources.

Despite the many beliefs and theories on the relevance of domestic structure to war, the relationship between the two has not been subjected to much empirical research. Because it is easy to observe democratic nations at war, the proposition does not seem intuitive to students of history. One such study, using a population of wars that is only modified here, categorized the political structures of nations going to war according to whether they were "bourgeois democratic" or non-democratic (Small and Singer, 1976). Since 1816, both kinds of regimes engaged in war in not significantly different numbers. Because only nations going to war were examined, no conclusion as to whether either type of political structure is more or less war-prone could be made, only that both types seemed equally likely to go to war (Small and Singer, 1976, p. 61). In addition, the codings were not based on any particular feature of the political system that might be related to decisions for war; merely the general characteristic of "democratic" institutions was used, based on the existence of freely elected public officials. Finally, no distinction was made between initiating a war and joining the belligerents of an ongoing war.

In a much more extensive research effort, Steve Chan sought to better establish the relationship between democracy and international violence (1984). In presenting a wide variety of analyses based on a dichotomous distinction between "more free" and "less free," Chan reported mixed findings. Following the recent arguments of Rudolph Rummel (1983), Chan found that a majority of wars in the late 1970s were conducted by "less free" governments, but the choice of time period can distort analyses (Weede, 1984). When the war experiences of all independent national governments were studied, a slightly negative relationship emerged, indicating that "more free" governments were a bit more likely to participate in interstate war. This is remarkably true for the 1946–72 period. However, Chan studied the number of years at war and not separate decisions for beginning a war. Accordingly, the many nation-years at war during the First World War, Second World War, and Korean War, in which very many "more free" nations joined after their onset, somewhat bias the results. Still, Chan's analyses support the connection of domestic structure to war, although in qualified terms.

Another line of research also indicated that regime type may be related to foreign-conflict behavior, defined more broadly than interstate war (Wilkenfeld, 1972). In analyses investigating the relationship between domestic and foreign conflict, no relationship could be found until regime type was included as an explanatory variable. For "polyarchic" (multiparty democracies) governments, domestic conflict was not found to be related to the level of foreign conflict, but "centrist" (single-party regimes) and "personalist" (authoritarian Third World regimes) governments were found to be more prone to foreign conflict.

The existing research incorporating features of the polity in analyses of foreign conflict and war have been suggestive of relationships, but far from definitive. The Chan study most clearly resembles the data and approach taken here, so if his mixed findings are to serve as a guide, one would expect to find no relationship between aspects of domestic political structure and decisions for war over the entire period in question. However, important relationships can be better examined by contrasting separate decisions for war.

ELEMENTS OF DOMESTIC POLITICAL STRUCTURE

There are many elements of domestic political structure, and, in their combination, they comprise the source and outcome of government policy. Every nation's domestic political structure is unique, but there are common elements that vary in degree and direction. The study of domestic political constraints on war should focus on these particular elements of domestic structure and not seek to categorize regimes too roughly. Indeed, if one wishes to use the standard of democracy or freedom, it is almost impossible to specify the necessary conditions that are suitable to normative concerns and change over time. One might, for example, make universal suffrage a criterion for democracy, which would limit its applicability to the United States until the 1920s and Switzerland until the 1970s. Constraints on decisions for war must take recognizable avenues to limit governmental choice.

As noted in chapter 2, domestic political constraints on foreign policy actions can occur in two aspects of domestic political structure: either within the broader domestic political system or inside government itself. Because it is nearly impossible consistently to identify and measure the influence that various organizations and individuals within the institutional or informative structure of government have on the actual conduct of government, this research will focus on the relationship between the extragovernmental sources of constraint and decisions for war, that is, on change in the domestic environment of central governments capable of waging war, not on decision-making itself.

Given this restriction, there are two avenues of domestic political constraint on decisions for war. In the absence of an absolute ruler or unlimited dictator, formal institutional constraints exist to restrict the actions of an effective chief executive as leader of the government. Such constraints are familiarly known as "checks and balances" between branches of government. In general terms, these constraints are posed by a legislature that exercises direct limits on the war-making abilities of an executive branch responsible for the conduct of foreign affairs.

On the other hand, the activity of groups and organizations seeking to advance the interests of particular segments of a society represent another sort of constraint on the actions of national political elites. Open political competition constitutes a second source of constraint on the actions of national governments considering war. The openness of a political system, especially in the area of electoral competition, creates an environment in which other priorities for government can dominate security interests.

LIMITS ON THE ACTIONS OF THE EXECUTIVE

Institutions that participate in the making of national policies are easy to observe because of their highly visible organizational presence and activities. Monarchies, cabinets, and legislatures function as public bodies. To measure the degree of their participation in the making of policy and to assess their role as a constraint on decisions for war, the activities of such institutions must be noted and compared. Across time and national governments, however, these institutional constraints are quite diverse in form and content. At one extreme, contemporary differences between the variety of nations with parliamentary systems—some with formal constitutions, some without—and nations with other forms of legislative participation are significant. At the other extreme, differences among nations with no rival institutions to the chief executive are also apparent. Further, it is difficult to distinguish the differences between nations with no pretense of a sanctioning legislature from those with a variety of symbolic or puppet bodies.

Because of this diversity of institutional arrangements, it is necessary to develop operational categories of institutional participation as indicators of the degree to which such bodies are able to constrain the actions of a chief executive, defined as the central ruling elite capable of initiating war. This is a formidable task that must eventually rely on judgmental codings of institutional configurations.

In research investigating a quite different theoretical question (the duration of various polities since 1800), Ted Robert Gurr has developed indicators of several features of each polity's political system (1974). One indicator is relevant to the hypothesis of interest here: the independence of executive authority. Gurr defines his measure of limits on the executive as "the extent of effective institutionalized limitations on executive authority. Such limitations may be imposed by any 'accountability group.' In Western democracies, these are usually legislatures. Other kinds of accountability groups are the ruling party in a one-party state; councils of nobles or powerful advisors in monarchies; and in many nations, a strong independent judiciary" (1978, p. 141).

Gurr examined each of the independent nations in the interstate system since 1800 and, on the basis of their respective political histories, coded their attributes in accord with his concept of the scope of executive authority. The four categories necessary to differentiate limits on the authority of the executive are defined and illustrated as follows (pp. 141–43):

Unlimited Authority. There are no regular limitations on the executive's actions (as distinct from irregular limitations such as the threat or actuality of coups and assassination). For example:

1. Constitutional restrictions on executive action are ignored.
2. Constitution is frequently revised or suspended at the executive's initiative.
3. There is no legislative assembly, OR it is called and dismissed at the executive's pleasure.

4. The executive appoints a majority of members of any accountability group and can remove them at will.
5. The legislature cannot initiate legislation or veto or suspend acts of the executive.
6. Rule by decree is repeatedly used.

If the executive is given limited or unlimited power by a representative body to cope with an emergency and relents this power after the emergency has passed, this is NOT a change to unlimited authority.

Slight to Moderate Limitations on Executive Authority. There are some real but limited restraints on the executive. For example:

1. The legislature initiates some categories of legislation.
2. The legislature delays implementation of executive acts or decrees.
3. The executive fails to change some constitutional restrictions, such as prohibitions of succeeding himself or extending his term.
4. The ruling party initiates some legislation or takes some administrative action independently of the executive.
5. There is an independent judiciary.

Substantial Limitations on Executive Authority. The executive has more effective authority than any accountability group, but is subject to substantial constraints by them. For example:

1. A legislature or party council often modifies or defeats executive proposals for action.
2. A council or legislature sometimes refuses funds to the executive.
3. The accountability groups make important appointments to administrative posts.
4. The legislature refuses the executive permission to leave the country.

77

Executive Parity or Subordination. Accountability groups have effective authority equal to or greater than the executive in most areas of activity. For example:

1. A legislature, ruling party, or council of nobles initiates much of the important legislation.
2. The executive (president, premier, king, queen, cabinet, council) is chosen by the accountability group AND is dependent on its continued support to remain in office (as in most parliamentary systems).
3. In multiparty systems, there is chronic cabinet instability.

Gurr's data exists for 144 independent governments extant during some part of the period since 1815. Three independent nations which Gurr excluded have been coded with the use of William Langer's *Encyclopedia of World History* (1972); they are Hesse-Darmstadt (moderate limits) and Hesse-Kassel and Mecklenburg-Schwerin (unlimited executive authority). Newly independent governments and several overlooked by Gurr are coded using the information supplied in Arthur Banks, *Political Handbook of the World* (1977).[1]

The unavailability of alternative measures of limitations on executive authority make it difficult to verify the accuracy of Gurr's codings. However, Gurr's codings can be compared with a similar measure presented in the *World Handbook of Political and Social Indicators* by Charles Lewis Taylor and Michael C. Hudson (1972, table 2-9, p. 57), which includes a four-level categorization of nations, placing them in groups according to their deviation from a "competitive and free norm." While the two scales are by no means intended to be identical, they seem to tap a common notion of political openness (gamma = .76).

The ordinal nature of Gurr's indicator of institutional constraints on the actions of policy-makers limits the number and kind of analyses appropriate to discovering valid empirical relationships. Spe-

1. *Legislative parity:* Bahamas, Barbados, Botswana, Fiji, Gambia, Grenada, Guyana, Laos (1954–59), Maldive Islands (1968–71), Malta, and Mauritius; *moderate limits:* Laos (1960–74), Maldive Islands (1972–75), Mongolia (1921–23); *unlimited executive:* Bahrain, Bangladesh, Guinea-Bissau, Laos (1975), Maldive Islands (1965–67), Mongolia (1924–75), Oman, Swaziland, United Arab Emirates, and the People's Democratic Republic of Yemen.

cifically, only contingency table analyses are appropriate. There are a variety of measures available to assess relationships, each with its own particular characteristics depending on the nature of the variables and the hypothesis being tested (see Weisberg, 1974). For a hypothesis for which the null hypothesis is the independence of two variables and for which the data has an uneven distribution (war, of which only a small percentage of independent governments decide for in any year) even fewer tests are available. Goodman and Kruskal's gamma statistic suits the purposes of the tests proposed here. Because of its treatment of ties, the gamma statistic is large compared to other statistics portraying relationships between ordinal variables. This is a desirable feature of the statistic for the questions posed here. In particular, gamma, which ranges in value from -1.00 to 1.00, will be 1.00 if *each* of the governments going to war in a given year has an executive with unlimited authority. Similarly, if each of the governments going to war in a given year possesses executive parity, the gamma will be -1.00. Other instances of gamma will be determined both by the distribution of governments deciding for war and according to the distribution of institutional constraints across all governments in that year.

Because these analyses deal with the population of independent national governments in every year in which interstate war occurs and not with a sample of governments, levels of statistical significance are not meaningful, because there is no need to generalize beyond to cases included in the analyses. The gamma statistic itself depicts the strength of relationship irrespective of the number of cases examined.

Table 4.1 shows the contingency tables obtained by comparing decisions for war with Gurr's codings of each nation's limits on the authority of the executive for each year in which an interstate war occurred between 1816 and 1975. A positive relationship indicates congruence with the hypothesis that greater limits on executive authority are associated with no decision of war. A negative relationship shows that the nations going to war are comparatively more limited than would be expected based on the distribution of executive limitations across the governments.

It is clear that no dominant relationship exists. Strong positive relationships consistent with the hypothesis of unlimited executives

TABLE 4.1 LIMITS ON EXECUTIVE AUTHORITY AND DECISIONS FOR WAR

Year	N	Decision	Unlimited Authority	Moderate Limits	Substantial Limits	Legislative Parity	Gamma
1823	23	War	0	2	0	0	−.44
		No War	13	3	2	3	
1828	25	War	2	0	0	0	1.00
		No War	14	4	2	3	
1846	35	War	1	0	0	1	−.32
		No War	17	8	6	2	
1848	37	War	4	0	0	0	1.00
		No War	15	9	6	3	
1849	38	War	2	0	1	1	−.12
		No War	13	13	5	3	
1851	39	War	2	0	0	0	1.00
		No War	15	13	6	3	
1853	39	War	2	0	0	0	1.00
		No War	15	14	5	3	
1856	41	War	1	0	0	1	−.29
		No War	19	13	4	3	
1859	42	War	4	1	0	0	.67
		No War	17	12	4	4	
1860	44	War	2	1	0	0	.43
		No War	20	12	4	5	
1862	39	War	2	0	0	0	1.00
		No War	15	13	4	5	
1863	39	War	1	1	0	0	.32
		No War	16	11	4	6	
1864	39	War	2	2	1	0	−.05
		No War	14	11	3	6	
1865	39	War	2	0	0	0	1.00
		No War	15	12	4	6	
1866	39	War	3	7	1	0	−.02
		No War	13	7	2	6	
1870	34	War	0	3	2	0	−.30
		No War	12	8	2	7	
1877	32	War	1	1	0	0	.57
		No War	9	9	2	10	

Table 4.1   *Continued*

Year	N	Decision	Unlimited Authority	Moderate Limits	Substantial Limits	Legislative Parity	Gamma
1879	34	War	1	0	1	0	.26
		No War	11	9	2	10	
1884	35	War	1	0	0	1	−.02
		No War	10	10	4	9	
1885	35	War	0	2	0	0	.12
		No War	11	8	4	10	
1894	38	War	1	0	0	1	.00
		No War	10	12	4	10	
1897	39	War	1	0	0	1	−.02
		No War	11	12	4	10	
1898	40	War	0	0	0	2	−1.00
		No War	13	12	4	9	
1904	43	War	1	0	0	1	−.03
		No War	12	13	5	10	
1906	43	War	2	1	0	0	.71
		No War	12	12	5	11	
1907	43	War	2	1	0	0	.71
		No War	12	12	5	11	
1909	44	War	1	0	0	1	−.03
		No War	13	13	5	11	
1911	43	War	1	1	0	0	.65
		No War	10	12	7	12	
1912	43	War	1	0	2	1	−.28
		No War	10	13	5	11	
1913	43	War	1	1	2	1	−.10
		No War	10	12	5	11	
1914	44	War	1	2	1	4	−.44
		No War	11	11	6	8	
1919	51	War	0	3	1	1	.12
		No War	8	13	7	18	
1920	61	War	0	1	0	1	−.16
		No War	11	15	9	24	

Continued on next page

Table 4.1 *Continued*

Year	N	Decision	Unlim-ited Authority	Moderate Limits	Substantial Limits	Legislative Parity	Gamma
1931	65	War	1	0	0	1	.06
		No War	18	15	7	23	
1932	66	War	1	1	0	0	.60
		No War	19	14	7	24	
1935	66	War	2	0	0	0	1.00
		No War	20	16	6	22	
1937	66	War	1	0	0	1	−.05
		No War	24	15	5	20	
1939	65	War	2	1	0	7	−.55
		No War	20	16	5	14	
1948	72	War	1	2	1	2	−.04
		No War	17	18	5	26	
1950	75	War	0	2	0	1	−.07
		No War	18	19	8	27	
1956	87	War	0	3	0	3	−.35
		No War	20	25	9	27	
1962	117	War	1	0	0	1	.03
		No War	28	39	15	33	
1965	124	War	2	1	0	2	.16
		No War	30	40	15	36	
1967	128	War	1	2	0	1	.10
		No War	36	34	17	37	
1969	131	War	0	1	1	0	−.13
		No War	41	36	13	39	
1971	135	War	0	1	0	1	−.46
		No War	45	36	15	37	
1973	137	War	1	1	0	1	−.03
		No War	48	36	13	37	
1974	139	War	0	0	1	1	−.65
		No War	50	36	12	39	

being more prone to war occur for some years, but negative or no relationship exists for others. In fact, if plus or minus .10 is used as a criterion of either a positive or negative relationship, only nineteen of forty-eight (42%) war years fit the hypothesized relationship. Sixteen (33%) fit the opposite negative hypothesis, and for twelve (25%) war years, governments going to war cannot be said to be either more or less restrictive of executive authority. In short, this analysis finds only very modest evidence that governments with more limits on executive authority tend to wage less war than do other governments.

A look at the separate war years shows that in seven years, only governments with unlimited executive authority decided for war: the Russo-Turkish Wars of 1828 and 1853 (Crimean), the two wars of 1848, the La Plata War of 1851, the Franco-Mexican War of 1862, the 1865 Spanish-Chilean War, and the 1935 Italo-Ethiopian War. Six additional years show a strong positive relationship: 1859, when two wars occurred (one of Italian unification and a Spanish-Moroccan war), the Russo-Turkish War of 1877, two Central American Wars (1906 and 1907), the Italo-Turkish War (1911), and the 1932 Chaco War. Four years tend in the positive direction: 1860, when two wars of Italian unification were fought; 1863, the Ecuador-Colombian War; 1879, the Pacific War; and 1965, the Indochina War and Kashmir wars.

Of these forty-three decisions for war by governments in years that fit the hypothesis, seventeen decisions for war were made by imperial governments: Piedmont/Italy (6 decisions for war, 10 if one also includes decisions by Rome and Sicily), Turkey (4), Imperial Russia (3 times against Turkey), Spain and France (2 each between 1859 and 1865). Most of Italy's record involves the four wars of unification between 1848 and 1860, but also includes war against Turkey and Ethiopia. The other Turkish war decisions were against Russia and part of a long series of imperial contests dating to the eighteenth century. It is noteworthy that both France and Spain had mixed records of democracy throughout the nineteenth century. In a short period of time when both had unlimited executive authority, each fought a war in Latin America (Chile and Mexico) and another closer to home (Morocco and Italy). Finally, sixteen decisions for war were made by Latin American governments, which maintained a spotty record of democracy. The remaining five decisions are divided among three European monarchies (Austria, Germany, and Denmark) and two African monarchies (Morocco and Ethiopia).

Two other wars also challenge the existence of a relationship between limits on authority and war. Only the Spanish-American War occurred between nations that both possessed governments with legislative parity (gamma = −1.00). The United States maintained stable democratic institutions, and although the extent of democracy was not as great in Spain, factional rivalry posed real limits on central authority. The 1974 Turkish-Cyprus War was fought between a Cypriot government with a strong legislature and a Turkish government that faced some limits from its parliament.

More troublesome is the case of the Second World War, when six parliamentary democracies (including four British dominions) went to war on behalf of undemocratic Poland against totalitarian Germany. Later in 1939, the Soviet Union decided on war against democratic Finland. One can make the Second World War fit the hypothesis only by reducing the war to its original two belligerents, Germany and Poland, which were both undemocratic. This poses the additional curiosity of why the United Kingdom and France would fight to defend undemocratic Poland and not democratic Czechoslovakia in 1938. Power politics would point to the security implications of each situation, noting that the German threat had grown over one year. A domestic-political-structure argument suggests that the subsequent collapse of Czech independence in the spring of 1939 removed domestic political constraints that had existed in the fall of 1938.

Although less so, World War I is also an exception to the hypothesis: the United Kingdom, France, Belgium, Serbia, and Japan had limited executive authority, whereas Germany, Austria, Hungary, and Russia did not. In this instance, only narrow focus on monarchical Austria's decision to attack Serbia rescues the hypothesis. Other wars contrary to the theoretical expectation are the Franco-Spanish War (1823), Mexican-American War (1846), Anglo-Persian War (1856), Franco-Prussian War (1870), and the Indo-Pakistani War (1971). Two wars occurred in the fall of 1956 when three parliamentary democracies went to war against Egypt and the Soviet Union invaded Hungary. The second war confirms the hypothesis, but the

Suez War makes 1956 another example of democratic governments deciding for war.

Of the war years that feature governments with legislative parity, forty-one decisions for war were taken. Five decisions were by France, although only three were taken in parliamentary periods (1914, 1939, and 1956). Four decisions were by the United Kingdom and two each by the United States and Spain in its more republican periods. Two German decisions (1914 and 1939) were against non-democratic governments that quickly acquired allies with parliamentary governments. The two Russian/Soviet decisions were in alliance with parliamentary governments against Germany (1914 and 1939). In the instance of Russian/Soviet decisions for war, power politics and security concerns seem to dominate any ideological preference. Similarly the domestic political structure of allies does not constrain decisions for war.

The distribution of decisions for war according to limits on executive authority only moderately supports the hypothesis that such constraints make the choice for war less likely. Limited governments do go to war, occasionally against each other (the Spanish-American War and the Turkish-Cyprus War). As democratic institutions have grown in number throughout the global system, this may not be surprising.

Since a major interest of this study is change over time, it is important to examine the relationships between limits on executive authority and decisions for war over time. Table 4.2 summarizes these trends derived from an ordinary least-squares regression of the gamma statistics on time for each of the five historical system epochs discussed in chapter 3.

It is clear that, over time, relationships become more negative, which shows that governments with comparatively more limitations made proportionately more decisions for war. In the later two periods, the relationship of the gamma statistics calculated for all war years are negative, whereas for the earlier periods, the hypothesized positive relationship is apparent. A markedly strong downward trend is exhibited in the period from 1850 to 1870. The wars of this period were predominantly wars of national unification on the part of Germany and Italy. The creation of these two larger nations was accomplished not so much by the coming together of

TABLE 4.2 TRENDS IN THE RELATIONSHIP BETWEEN LIMITS ON EXECUTIVE AUTHORITY AND DECISIONS FOR WAR

Period	N	Decision	Limits				Gamma	Slope	r^2
			None	Few	Many	All			
1816–1849	158	War	9	2	1	2	.18	.003	.00
		No War	72	37	21	14			
1850–1870	434	War	20	15	4	1	.19	−.048	.23
		No War	191	138	46	59			
1871–1914	514	War	14	9	6	13	−.03	−.007	.04
		No War	155	157	61	141			
1919–1939	415	War	7	6	1	11	−.08	.002	.00
		No War	120	104	46	145			
1946–1975	1112	War	6	12	3	12	−.15	−.008	.07
		No War	333	319	122	338			

separate governments with a common background as by the establishment of the domination of a single government—those of Prussia and Piedmont. In each instance, these governments possessed less domestic limitation on their monarchical orders than their compatriot national governments, which were eliminated in the process.

Trends, as indicated by the regression slope coefficients shown in table 4.2, also reflect an increasingly negative relationship. The slope coefficient, the value of which is the annual change in the value of the gamma statistic, is negative for the pre–World War I and post–World War II periods and mostly flat or slightly increasing for the other periods. Not surprisingly, a straight line does not describe trends very well as would be expected and as described by the r^2 statistic, but it does accurately describe the trend within each period (if for only a few war years). For the period as a whole, the trend is negative with a slope of −.003 (r^2 = .08). When divided into two parts at the First World War, both periods show a declining trend, −.003 and −.007 (r^2 = .02 and .12) respectively.

The absence of strong relationships in these analyses makes conclusions elusive. Two things may be said, however. First, based on these limited analyses, no solid relationship exists between limits on the independence of the chief executive and decisions for war, although there is a modest pattern. Independent governments with limits do not appear to be significantly less prone to such actions. The very mixed nature of the gamma statistics bear this out.

Secondly, although trends are not marked, as time goes on it appears as though governments *with* limits on executive authority are increasingly *more* inclined to go to war. This conclusion is based on the small trends exhibited by fitting linear trends to the gamma statistics. Both conclusions, however, will need to be further examined in the context of other factors considered later.

POLITICAL COMPETITION AND DECISIONS FOR WAR

Measuring non-institutional constraints on national policy-makers is substantially more problematic than measuring formal institutional constraints. The many groups and organizations that seek to influence a central government are considerably more diverse, both in their composition and in the means by which they operate in the realm of domestic politics. Whereas formal political institutions are fairly easy to identify, it is often difficult to observe interest groups in a polity, let alone measure their effect on governments and policy-making.

Several indicators of societal political participation, such as unionization, enfranchisement and electoral turnout, and political party membership and activity, can be used to construct measures. Unfortunately, such data does not exist for a sufficient number of political systems for a long enough period of time to make them useful to this study. Perhaps more importantly, these indicators reflect political activities that are different in each polity. Cross-national indicators can be misleading, given the different roles played by such groups in society.

Once again, judgmental codings of political participation are necessary, and an indicator developed by Ted Robert Gurr to measure the extent of political competition and opposition in a polity can be used. Gurr lists five categories of competition (1978, pp. 143–45):

Suppressed or Nonexistent Competition. No significant political oppositional activity of any kind is permitted outside the ranks of the regime and the governing party—if there is one.

Restricted Competition. Some organized, competitive political activity occurs outside government, without serious factionalism; but the regime in power systematically and sharply limits competitive political activity in form and/or extent, or in ways that exclude substantial groups (20 percent or more of the male adult population) from participation. Large classes of people, groups, or types of peaceful political participation are systematically, persistently, and continuously excluded from the political process. Examples are:

1. Prohibiting some kinds of political organizations, either by type or groups of people involved (for example, no national political parties or no political organizations among blacks or Peronistas).
2. Prohibiting some kinds of political action (for example, Communist parties may organize but are prohibited from competing in elections).
3. Systematic harassment of political opposition (leaders are killed, jailed, or sent into exile; opposition media—press, radio stations—are banned, and so forth).

Uninstitutional Competition. Political competition is fluid; there are no enduring national political organizations and no systematic regime controls on political activity. Political groupings tend to form around particular leaders, regional interests, religions, or ethnic or clan groups; but the number and relative importance of such groups in national political life varies substantially over time. Uninstitutionalized competition may or may not be charcterized by violent conflict among partisan groups.

Factional/Restricted Competition. Relatively stable and enduring political groups which compete for political influence at the national level—but the competition among them is intense, hostile, and frequently violent. Extreme factional competition may be manifest in the establishment of rival governments in civil war. When one such group emerges on top, it typically restricts its opponents' political activities; hence the polity is factional/restricted by turns. Also coded here are polities in which political groups are factional but a part or most of the population is excluded from political competition (for example, Indians in some South American countries until recently).

Institutional Competition. Relatively stable and enduring political groups which regularly compete for political influence on the national level; competition seldom causes widespread violence or disruption. The regime usually regulates their activity, but no significant political groups are suppressed or systematically excluded from competition. Very small parties or political groups may be restricted in the institutional-competition pattern.

As with the indicator of executive authority, this measure can be compared with that of the *World Handbook of Political and Social Indicators* as a check on its reliability. Gurr's measure of political competition is even more correlated with that for limits on executive authority (gamma = .84) and also indicates that his ordinal scale reflects an identifiable feature of these political systems.

With these codings of polities according to domestic political competition, analyses can be conducted along the lines of those for limits on executive authority.[2] Since two of the categories, uninstitutional and factional/restricted competition, are distinguished only by the level of domestic violence, they are combined for the following analyses. In addition, there are never more than three polities with uninstitutional competition in any one year. As in the examination of limits on executive authority, analyses can be conducted with a four-level ordinal variable of political competition. Table 4.3 lists the findings for each war year.

As was the case in analyses of relationships between decisions

2. *Institutional competition:* Bahamas, Barbados, Botswana, Fiji, Gambia, Grenada, Guyana, Laos (1954–59), Maldive Islands (1968–71), Malta, Mauritius (1968–70); *factional competition:* Bangladesh, Laos (1960–74), Mauritius (1971–75); *restricted competition:* Lesotho, Maldive Islands (1965–67, 1972–75), Mongolia (1921–23), Swaziland (1968–72), Hesse-Darmstadt; *suppressed competition:* Bahrain, Guinea-Bissau, Laos (1975), Mongolia (1924–75), Oman, Swaziland (1973–75), United Arab Emirates, South Yemen, Hesse-Kasel, Mecklenburg.

TABLE 4.3   DOMESTIC POLITICAL COMPETITION AND DECISIONS FOR
WAR

| Year | N | Decision | Type of Competition | | | | Gamma |
			Suppressed	Restricted	Factional	Institutional	
1823	23	War	0	0	2	0	−.89
		No War	12	6	2	1	
1828	25	War	2	0	0	0	1.00
		No War	10	6	6	1	
1846	35	War	0	0	1	1	−.92
		No War	12	8	11	2	
1848	37	War	3	1	0	0	.81
		No War	9	7	14	3	
1849	38	War	1	0	2	1	−.34
		No War	7	11	13	3	
1851	39	War	0	0	2	0	−.67
		No War	9	11	13	4	
1853	39	War	2	0	0	0	1.00
		No War	7	12	14	4	
1856	41	War	1	0	0	1	−.12
		No War	10	10	17	2	
1859	42	War	0	2	3	0	−.26
		No War	10	9	15	3	
1860	44	War	2	1	0	0	.84
		No War	8	10	20	3	
1862	39	War	0	1	1	0	.11
		No War	5	10	19	3	
1863	39	War	0	0	2	0	−.68
		No War	5	11	18	3	
1864	39	War	1	2	1	1	−.15
		No War	4	9	19	2	
1865	39	War	0	0	2	0	−.70
		No War	6	11	17	3	
1866	39	War	2	7	2	0	.63
		No War	4	4	17	3	
1870	34	War	0	5	0	0	.69
		No War	4	3	19	3	
1877	32	War	1	0	1	0	.63
		No War	3	4	19	4	

Table 4.3 *Continued*

Year	N	Decision	Type of Competition				Gamma
			Suppressed	Restricted	Factional	Institutional	
1879	34	War	1	0	1	0	.52
		No War	4	6	18	4	
1884	35	War	0	0	2	0	−.43
		No War	4	6	19	4	
1885	35	War	0	0	2	0	−.43
		No War	4	6	19	4	
1894	38	War	0	0	2	0	−.23
		No War	5	3	23	5	
1897	39	War	1	0	0	1	.00
		No War	4	3	26	4	
1898	40	War	0	0	0	2	−1.00
		No War	5	3	27	3	
1904	43	War	1	0	1	0	.64
		No War	5	4	27	5	
1906	43	War	1	1	1	0	.70
		No War	5	3	25	7	
1907	43	War	0	1	2	0	.42
		No War	5	2	26	7	
1909	44	War	0	0	2	0	.00
		No War	5	3	26	8	
1911	43	War	0	1	1	0	.35
		No War	3	2	26	8	
1912	43	War	0	1	1	2	−.12
		No War	5	2	26	6	
1913	43	War	0	1	2	2	−.32
		No War	5	2	25	6	
1914	44	War	0	0	6	2	−.50
		No War	5	3	22	6	
1919	51	War	0	1	4	0	.52
		No War	4	1	32	9	
1920	61	War	0	0	2	0	.23
		No War	6	4	33	16	
1931	65	War	0	0	2	0	−.14
		No War	15	9	21	18	

Continued on next page

Table 4.3 *Continued*

Year	N	Decision	Type of Competition				Gamma
			Suppressed	Restricted	Factional	Institutional	
1932	66	War	0	0	2	0	− .14
		No War	16	8	22	18	
1935	66	War	2	0	0	0	1.00
		No War	18	8	21	17	
1937	66	War	0	0	2	0	− .29
		No War	21	10	16	17	
1939	65	War	2	3	0	5	− .17
		No War	16	5	20	14	
1948	72	War	0	1	4	1	.04
		No War	14	6	21	25	
1950	75	War	1	1	0	1	.22
		No War	16	9	25	22	
1956	87	War	3	0	0	3	.01
		No War	22	12	24	23	
1962	117	War	1	0	0	1	− .08
		No War	41	14	32	28	
1965	124	War	1	0	2	2	− .43
		No War	43	14	31	33	
1967	128	War	2	0	1	1	.12
		No War	46	16	26	36	
1969	131	War	0	0	1	1	− .60
		No War	53	13	24	39	
1971	135	War	0	0	0	2	− 1.00
		No War	58	13	24	38	
1973	137	War	1	0	1	1	− .19
		No War	60	11	24	39	
1974	139	War	0	0	1	1	− .62
		No War	62	12	23	40	

for war and limits on the authority of the executive, no clear patterns emerge—only some years fit the hypothesis of decisions for war being related to less political competition. Unlike the previous analysis, however, more war years contradict the hypothesis. Out of forty-eight war years, twenty-five (52%) show a negative relationship. In these instances, the independent governments going to war possess more domestic political competition than those not at war. Only eighteen (37%) fit the hypothesis of a positive relationship, and five (11%) war years show no significant difference between governments going to war along distinctions of political competition.

Turning first to the seventeen wars that clearly support the hypothesis that political competition constrains decisions for war: three war years occurred when only governments that suppressed opposition decided for war—the Russo-Turkish Wars of 1828 and 1853 (Crimean) and the Italo-Ethiopian War of 1935. The two Italian Wars of Unification in 1860 also match the hypothesis, since Rome allowed restricted political competition whereas Piedmont and Sicily suppressed it. Another ten war years also support the hypothesis: the Austro-Piedmont and Prusso-Danish Wars (1848), Seven Weeks War (1866), Franco-Prussian War (1870), Russo-Turkish War (1877), Pacific War (1879), Russo-Japanese War (1904), two Central American Wars (1906 and 1907), Italo-Ethiopian War (1911), and the two wars of 1919, between Hungary and the Allies and between Greece and Turkey. The Soviet-Polish War of 1920 is only slightly supportive of the hypothesis because both new governments permitted factional political competition.

In contrast to the analyses for limits on executive authority, fewer wars fit the hypothesis. Seven wars with positive gamma coefficients in the previous analysis are negative or near zero, which depicts a general trend for political competition to advance more extensively than limits on authority. In other words, the distribution of political competition shows that governments are somewhat more prone to allow political opposition than direct limits on governmental authority. Four war years are added to the list of positive relationships: Seven Weeks (1866), Franco-Prussian (1870), Russo-Japanese (1904), and the two wars of 1919. For these five wars, governmental authority was more limited, but political competition restricted or suppressed.

The forty-four decisions for war that suit the hypothesis are concentrated somewhat differently than for limits on executive authority. As before, Russia, Turkey, and Italy lead with four each. Prussia made two decisions for war (1866 and 1870). The Italian and German Wars of Unification also involved smaller states—Sicily, Rome, and a total of twelve separate decisions for war by the German states. The remaining sixteen decisions for war comprise eight Latin American governments and Austria (1866), France (1870), Japan (1904), Hungary (1919), Romania (1919), Czechoslovakia (1919), Greece (1919), and Ethiopia (1935).

Thirteen war years stand out as markedly contrary to the hypothesized relationship. In these instances, governments with domestic structures that support political competition decided for war. The extreme cases are the Spanish-American War (1898) and Indo-Pakistani War (1971), when both governments at war existed with domestic political competition. Also in this category are the Franco-Spanish (1823) and Mexican-American Wars (1846). Strongly negative relationships exist for the La Plata (1851), Ecuador-Colombian (1863), Spanish-Chilean (1865), Football (1969), and Turko-Cyprus wars (1974). Less strongly, negative relationships exist for the War of the Roman Republic (1849), Sino-French War (1884), Central American War (1885), and World War I (1914).

Only six war years with negative relationships overlap with war years in that status for analysis of limits of executive authority: the Spanish-American (1898), Mexican-American (1846), Franco-Spanish (1823), Turkish-Cyprus (1974), Indo-Pakistani, and First World Wars (1914). These wars stand out as six cases when the governments to decide for war were open, when compared to other governments in that year, in the limitations placed on executive authority and the institutionalization of political competition.

The thirty-eight decisions for war in these instances of greater political competition contain four French, three Spanish, and two U.S. decisions for war at times of greater political competition. Non-competitive opponents include three Austrian and two German decisions. The remaining decisions for war are distributed

TABLE 4.4   TRENDS IN THE RELATIONSHIP BETWEEN DOMESTIC
POLITICAL COMPETITION AND DECISIONS FOR WAR

			Type of Competition						
Period	N	Decision	Sup-pressed	Re-stricted	Fac-tional	Institu-tional	Gamma	Slope	r^2
1816–1849	158	War	6	1	5	2	−.06	.001	.00
		No War	50	58	46	10			
1850–1870	434	War	8	17	13	2	.23	−.009	.01
		No War	78	112	208	36			
1871–1914	514	War	5	4	24	9	−.11	−.007	.03
		No War	64	50	327	73			
1919–1939	415	War	4	4	12	4	.01	−.019	.11
		No War	96	45	165	109			
1946–1975	1112	War	9	2	9	13	−.21	−.029	.47
		No War	415	120	254	323			

across twenty-three governments, including the United Kingdom, Russia, Italy, Turkey, and Japan.

There are an additional thirteen war years that show negative relationships, but only weakly so. Overall, the greater spread of political competition over legislative parity accounts for an even more neutral finding.

Trends in these relationships are also more negative than for limits on executive authority. Table 4.4 displays trends according to five historical periods.

As seen before, relationships are increasingly negative over time; the post–World War II period shows a clear (and statistically significant) downward trend. Since the end of World War II, wars tend increasingly to involve independent governments with greater degrees of political competition. For the period as a whole, the trend is slightly downward, −.002 (r^2 = .02), as indicated by results of a regression of gamma statistics against time. Most of this downward trend is found in the most recent period, of course, as a division of the period at World War I produces little downward trend before 1914, −.001 (r^2 = .00) and a considerable decline since 1919, −.014

($r^2 = .35$). In two periods, 1850–1970 and 1919–39, the trends in relationships are increasingly negative, indicating that while the relationships themselves may fit the hypothesis as a whole, as time passes this relationship becomes weaker. Interestingly, each of these periods is marked by the increasing frequency of war over the course of time.

The analyses of political competition are different from those of executive authority in that relationships tend to be more negative, because even fewer war years fit the hypothesized relationship of less political competition to decisions of war. What is perhaps most marked is the large and increasingly negative relationship in the period since World War II. Such mixed findings lead to a conclusion that no strong relationship exists, pending additional investigation.

POLITICAL COMPETITION AND LIMITS ON EXECUTIVE AUTHORITY

The analyses of two elements of domestic political structure were mainly consistent with each other, but not with what was expected on the basis of the theoretical reasoning developed earlier. In both analyses, many cases did not fit the hypothesis that independent governments with more open domestic structures are less likely to decide for war. In the case of political competition, however, contrary results were found in more war years than not. When trends are analyzed, both sets of analyses show that as time has passed, nations with more open domestic structures have been more prominent in the onset of war.

Despite the similarity of findings, the two indicators are different, as indeed they should be if they are intended to measure separate elements of domestic structure. Most war years show different degrees or kinds of relationship. This raises the question of whether a composite indicator of the two will produce substantially different results. Could it be that only governments that are constrained by *both* limits on the executive and open political competition are less inclined to decide for war?

Table 4.5 shows the interrelation of the two elements of domestic political structure. The relationship of the two is fairly patterned, with 71 percent of the nation-years falling on the diagonal of unlim-

TABLE 4.5   POLITICAL COMPETITION AND LIMITS ON EXECUTIVE
AUTHORITY

Political Competition	Limits on Authority			
	Unlimited Authority	Moderate Limits	Substantial Limits	Legislative Parity
Suppressed	1695	416	131	0
Restricted	206	534	266	187
Factional	913	1340	438	581
Institutional	0	114	116	1528

N = 8465

ited/suppressed to limited/institutional, if values in the four center cells are treated as one.

Several composite indicators can be constructed. Here, a five-level ordinal measure is constructed by ordering the cases as follows:

1. Unlimited authority and suppressed competition.
2. Unlimited authority and restricted or factional competition, or suppressed competition and moderately or substantially limited authority.
3. Moderately or substantially limited authority and restricted or factional competition.
4. Legislative parity and restricted or factional competition, or institutional competition and moderately or substantially limited authority.
5. Legislative parity and institutional competition.

Variants on this scale are possible, especially seven-level scales designating either limits of executive authority or political competition as more important. To avoid such a choice, off-diagonal combinations are simply coded either two or four.

It makes very little difference, however, in analyses using this measure of political participation in its relation to decisions for war. In almost every war year, this composite measure of political participation is a sort of average between the two other indicators. In short, little is gained by combining the effects of these two sources of political participation.

Other insights might be gained by analyzing changes in domestic structure before war years. Could it be that governments going to war have recently modified levels of political participation? This question is unfortunately impossible to examine because of the limited nature of the four-level scales used to measure features of each polity. Political structures change so rarely that only a small portion (never more than three) change in any five-year period prior to war. What weak relationships exist are produced by the one or two exhibiting recent change.

ISSUES IN DISPUTE AND DECISIONS FOR WAR

Thus far, the results of analyses have not supported the theoretical arguments that have guided them: domestic political structure does not seem to be consistently related to decisions for war and, to the degree it is, it is related in the opposite direction than anticipated—over time, governments with more open domestic structures tend to decide for war slightly more often. This relationship has tended to be more negative in later periods, contrary to hypothesized notions of change.

These findings are, however, suggestive of further analyses that may elucidate more precisely the nature of the relationships. For example, it has been argued that wars occurring in more recent times are different from earlier ones as to the disputed issue or conflict of interest over which they are fought (Brodie, 1973; Howard, 1972). The changing nature of the disputes leading to war would seem to be related to the relevance of domestic structure to decisions for war. Could it be that more open political structures are prone to only particular types of war?

A simple coding of the nature of the dispute over which wars are fought can be used to examine this question, if in only a cursory way. By using an uncomplicated initial categorization of wars, an analysis is possible that may be revealing as to the relation of dispute issue to the questions examined here (see Wright, 1942). Unfortunately, categorizations of this sort have not been used frequently, but in examinations of the issues over which governments decide to go to war, three general categories can be discerned:

1. *Wars of Conquest.* Wars fought in order for one or more governments to take advantage of or to protect particular concessions in another nation. Such wars can range from overt aggression to actions to establish dominion over territory or resources in particular territory.
2. *Wars of Regime.* Wars fought over the right of particular elites to govern. Wars of succession and interventions in civil wars are examples.
3. *Wars of Legitimacy.* Wars fought over a disagreement in the rights of governments or some issue calling into question principles of the conduct of international relations. Irredentist or national liberation movements are prominent in this category, as are wars resulting from boundary disputes or the treatment of particular minorities in another nation.

All the wars examined here can be categorized according to these three types of interstate war (see table 4.6).[3] Using these categories of war, relationships can be examined with reference to type of war. It should be noted at the outset that these codings require refinement in order to merit confidence in research findings using them. To conduct additional detailed research into each war is far beyond the scope of this study. Thus, simply following the definitions outlined above, seventeen wars fall into the category of wars of conquest, thirty-six wars can be considered wars of legitimacy, and eight wars can be seen to have been fought over the existence of particular regimes.

It is now possible to compare the gamma statistics acquired in analyses assessing the relationships of limits on executive authority and political competition to decisions for war. In five years between 1816 and 1925, two different types of war occurred. In each instance (1848, 1859, 1912, 1919, and 1965), a gamma statistic for each war is used. Because further division of the forty-eight war years makes

3. The coding of each war by type is taken from the information supplied by Wright, *A Study of War* (1942) and Langer, *Encyclopedia of World History* (1972), and Day, *Border and Territorial Disputes* (1982). In ambiguous cases, the references cited in Small and Singer (1982) were consulted.

99

TABLE 4.6   INTERSTATE WARS CATEGORIZED BY ISSUE TYPE

Wars of Conquest

Russo-Turkish (1828)	Russian expansion to mouth of Danube, Abkhazia, Poti, and Achalzich
Crimean (1853)	Russian expansion in Danube principalities
Spanish-Moroccan (1859)	Expansion of Spanish enclaves in Morocco
French-Mexican (1862)	Establishment of French hegemony in Mexico
Lopez (1864)	Expansion of Paraguayan territory
Pacific (1879)	Chilean acquisition of Bolivia's Atacama Province
Sino-French (1884)	Expansion of French Empire in Indochina
Sino-Japanese (1894)	Expansion of Japanese Empire in China
Russo-Japanese (1904)	Russian and Japanese rivalry for Korea and Manchuria
Spanish-Morocco (1909)	Expansion of Spanish enclaves in Morocco
Italo-Turkish (1911)	Expansion of Italian Empire in Tripoli
World War I (1914)	Annexation of Serbia into Austria-Hungary
Manchurian (1931)	Expansion of Japanese Empire in China
Italo-Ethiopian (1935)	Expansion of Italian Empire in Ethiopia
Sino-Japanese (1937)	Expansion of Japanese Empire in China
World War II (1939)	Expansion of Germany in Poland
Russo-Finnish War (1939)	Annexation of Finnish territory to USSR

Wars of Regime

Franco-Spanish (1823)	Removal of constitutional (liberal) government and restoration of Ferdinand VII
Roman Republic (1849)	Removal of republican government (Mazzini) and restoration of Pope Pius IX
La Plata (1851)	Removal of Rosas government by allied forces led by Urquiza
Ecuadorian-Colombian (1863)	Colombian attempt to overthrow Flores government in Ecuador
Franco-Prussian (1870)	Hohenzollern succession to Spanish crown
Russo-Hungarian (1956)	Removal of Nagy government in Hungary
Uganda-Tanzania (1978)	Removal of Amin government in Uganda
Cambodia-Vietnam (1978)	Removal of Pol Pot government in Cambodia

Wars of Legitimacy

Mexican-American (1846)	Competing claims for Texas
Austro-Piedmont (1848)	Unification of Lombardy with Piedmont
First Schleswig-Holstein (1848)	Incorporation of Schleswig into the Kingdom of Denmark

TABLE 4.6 *Continued*

Anglo-Persian (1856)	Boundaries of Persia and Afghanistan
Italian (1859)	Liberation and federation of Italian Kingdoms according to the Plombieres agreement
Italo-Roman (1860)	Unification of Papal States with Piedmont
Italo-Sicilian (1860)	Unification of Kingdom of the Two Sicilies
Second Schleswig-Holstein (1864)	Incorporation of Schleswig into the Kingdom of Denmark
Spanish-Chilean (1865)	Spanish challenge to independence of Chile
Seven Weeks (1866)	Status of Holstein in German Confederation
Russo-Turkish (1877)	Russian support of revolts in the Balkans
Central American (1885)	Status and membership of Central American Federation
Greco-Turkish (1897)	Status of Macedonia and Crete
Spanish-American (1898)	Independence of Cuba
Central American (1906)	Status and membership of Central American Federation
Central American (1907)	Status and membership of Central American Federation
First Balkan (1912)	Boundaries of Turkey in Balkan Peninsula
Second Balkan (1913)	Boundaries of Bulgaria in Balkan Peninsula
Hungarian-Allies (1919)	Boundaries of Hungary
Greco-Turkish (1919)	Status of Greek territories around the Aegean according to Treaty of Sevres
Soviet-Polish (1920)	Boundaries of Poland
Chaco (1932)	Boundaries of Paraguay
Palestine (1949)	Boundaries and status of Israel
Korean (1950)	Unification and status of Korea
Sinai (1956)	Status of Suez Canal
Sino-Indian (1962)	Boundary between India and China
Kashmir (1965)	Indo-Pakistani border in Kashmir
Indochina (1965)	Unification and status of Vietnam
Six Day (1967)	Boundaries and status of Israel
Football (1969)	Boundary between El Salvador and Honduras
Indo-Pakistani (1971)	Independence of Bangladesh
Yom Kippur (1973)	Boundaries and status of Israel
Cyprus (1974)	Status of ethnic Turks in Cyprus
Ogaden (1977)	Unification of Ogaden with Somalia
Iran-Iraq (1979)	Boundary along Shatt al Arab
Falklands (1982)	Unification of Malvinas with Argentina

TABLE 4.7   POLITICAL PARTICIPATION AND WAR BY TYPE

War Type	Limits on Authority	Political Competition
Conquest	.39	.23
Regime	.15	− .15
Legitimacy	.08	− .12
Eta²	.10	.12

for many historical periods when only one type of war is present or too few for comparison, analysis by subperiods is misleading. For the period as a whole, however, several interesting conclusions can be made. Table 4.7 shows the results of analyses of variance of the gamma statistics derived earlier for the two indicators of political participation. The cell entries are the mean gamma statistics for each variable for the fifty-six wars between 1816 and 1975.

As has been the case in other analyses using the gamma statistics from contingency table analysis that have a tendency to vary widely, little variance is accounted for as indicated by the Eta² co-efficient. Despite this, the mean gamma scores for different types of war show that governments fighting wars of conquest are much more likely to have closed political structures than governments fighting wars of legitimacy or regime. This is particularly evident in the case of political competition where there is a difference of .38 (19% of the range between − 1.00 and 1.00) between wars of conquest and legitimacy and a difference of .35 (17%) between wars of conquest and wars of regime.

This helps to account for the increasingly negative relationships found in the previous analyses examining trends in relationships. Very few recent wars have been wars of conquest—in fact, no war from World War II to the present is categorized as such. If governments with more open domestic structures are more likely to fight wars of legitimacy or regime, and these wars predominate later in the period under examination, then it is no wonder that increasingly negative relationships result from the bivariate analyses of war years.

It is only in wars of conquest that an initiator or aggressive belligerent can be unambiguously identified. The analysis of war types indicates that invaders are likely to have more closed domestic political structures, and this, indeed, is the case. Table 4.8 shows that seventeen decisions for war of conquest were undertaken by invaders with closed political structures. Although six decisions to invade were by governments with legislative parity, no decision to wage war of conquest was taken by a government with institutionalized political competition. Those governments with legislative parity are marked by factional political competition. Four of these decisions were by Japan, where the constitution of 1890 quickly evolved to permit the diet to limit the authority of the emperor. The competition for leadership among contending political factions often influenced foreign affairs, especially actions in China. In the 1930s, the military used its ability to independently create conflict in China to undermine civilian opposition. After the beginning of war in 1937, the military moved to eliminate civilian control and the influence of the diet.

DECISIONS FOR WAR SINCE 1975

With the exception of the Falklands War between dictatorial Argentina and the democratic United Kingdom, the decisions for war since 1975 support the hypothesis of closed domestic structure and war. Wars between Ethiopia and Somalia (1977), Cambodia and Vietnam (1978), Uganda and Tanzania (1978), and Iran and Iraq (1980) were all contests between governments with unlimited authority and restricted or suppressed political competition. The Ugandan, Cambodian, Argentinian, Ethiopian, and Iranian governments were notorious for their persecution of domestic opponents, which makes the regime dimension important in each war, although only the Uganda-Tanzania and Cambodia-Vietnam wars are coded as wars of regime.

With the exception of the British decision to fight the Falklands War, the wars since 1975 reverse the trend toward more democratic governments deciding for war. In these five wars, decidedly undemocratic governments waged war, which points out the impor-

TABLE 4.8   DOMESTIC POLITICAL STRUCTURE OF INVADERS IN WARS OF
CONQUEST

Invader	Year	Limits on Executive Authority	Political Competition
Russia	1828	Unlimited	Suppressed
Russia	1853	Unlimited	Suppressed
Spain	1859	Unlimited	Factional
France	1862	Unlimited	Factional
Paraguay	1864	Unlimited	Suppressed
Chile	1879	Unlimited	Suppressed
France	1884	Legislative parity	Factional
Japan	1894	Legislative parity	Factional
Japan	1904	Legislative parity	Factional
Spain	1909	Legislative parity	Factional
Italy	1911	Moderate limits	Restricted
Austria	1914	Unlimited	Restricted
Japan	1931	Legislative parity	Factional
Italy	1935	Unlimited	Suppressed
Japan	1937	Legislative parity	Factional
Germany	1939	Unlimited	Suppressed
Soviet Union	1939	Moderate limits	Suppressed

tance of time frame and overall trend. If one only studied the wars since 1975, one could draw a restrictive conclusion that was not consistent with the broader post–World War II period.

Further, the war between Argentina and the United Kingdom over the Falklands in 1982 demonstrates how the potential constraints of domestic structure can be overcome. The United Kingdom is among the oldest and most stable democracies in the global system, and although many in parliament opposed war at the time, the Thatcher government was firm in its intentions and received widespread public support. The domestic political cost of the decision for war seems to have come afterward, when open challenge to its actions cast doubt on the objectives and honesty of the Thatcher government. When one recalls the frequency of governmental change introduced by U.K. war involvement, one might conclude that heavy costs of U.K. decisions for war occur only after decision for war.

NATIONAL INTEREST VERSUS TENURE IN OFFICE

These results are strongly dependent on the coding of wars by type and, therefore, any conclusions drawn here should be labeled as tentative. Nonetheless, they are evidence of the importance of domestic political structure to decisions for war. It seems that a government constrained by the need to acquire the support of rival institutions and domestic interest groups would find it more difficult to mobilize support and resources for wars designed to extend the national interests through wars of conquest. Similarly, wars fought over disputed "rights" of governments may be the result of the relatively easier task of mobilizing support for "nationalistic" or legitimate causes. In fact, such actions may be used by political elites to advance their own domestic political cause. With that in mind, we should recall Kissinger's observation that power politics requires domestic structures that can support ruthlessness. This seems clearly true in the cases of wars of conquest, which most closely match the power-politics objective of expansion, but does not seem suitable to wars of legitimacy or regime, which tend to be fought by more democratic governments.

We should consider, therefore, replacing the lore of power politics with a law of politics: political elites wish to attain and stay in office. If political elites can use war to dominate domestic political structures, they will undoubtedly do so, as the Japanese military did in the 1930s. Similarly, political elites in government will fight war if it will extend or protect their tenure in office. This is obviously true of the direct external challenges in wars of regime; it may also be the case when democratic governments find that war is necessary to meet demands of legitimacy that may jeopardize tenure in office. For example, the Argentinian junta's decision to attack the Falklands was more related to the domestic political challenge it faced than to desire for power. If the junta had wanted more certainty of victory (the calculation of the probabilities of success), it would have delayed invasion several months. The Thatcher government, for its part, after three years in office, had fallen well behind in opinion polls. The decision to fight by both governments matches the requirements of rule more than the need for power and security.

Whether derived from the lore of power politics or the law of politics, the outcome of decision for war is the same. What is different is the assumed source of motivation. National interest serves theories of power politics, but the desire for tenure in office seems to hold a richer source of explanation and would encourage further investigation into domestic political structure and war.

5

FOREIGN TRADE
AND THE ONSET OF WAR

As we have seen, an open domestic political structure is limited as an effective constraint on the propensity of independent national governments to wage war. The theoretical arguments advanced in chapter 2 posited that one particularly important domestic interest group—business elites that profit from foreign trade—is a significant determinant of domestic political structure and may be especially effective in restricting the war-making abilities of national governments. This is the legacy of liberalism, which in the nineteenth century galvanized the political interest of industrialists and helped transform the structure of government and interests in foreign policy.

The source of the foreign-trade constraint on central government is threefold. First, because of the economic costs of disrupting foreign trade by war and the resulting realignment of national economies necessary to allocate resources for war ends, government is likely to be less inclined to accept the expense in terms of lost trade profits and economic growth, which may generate long-term disruption. This is a limitation found in the vulnerability produced by trade interdependence.

Second, the domestic interest group that benefits most from the profits of uninhibited international commerce represents an active and usually influential element of a political system. Depending on the size of the profits they stand to lose and their relative effectiveness in determining national policy, business elites involved in foreign trade may attempt to constrain government's war involvement. This constraint is produced by the interpenetration of nations by commercial business elites.

Third, the machinery of national government has changed to incorporate the interests of foreign trade, so that the goal of security must compete with interests more concerned with the condition of the national economy—a confusion of objectives that increases to the extent that economic well-being is linked to national security. As the government increases its role in the management of the national economy and international forces make a larger impact on economic performance, national government must take more responsibility for the maintenance of foreign trade. In this way, economic interests quite different from those of traditional diplomacy and defense are incorporated into the government's foreign-policy-making structure. The third constraint on decisions for war results from the interconnection of national economies and the governments responsible for them.

This chapter analyzes the empirical relationship of foreign trade to decisions for war. If any one of the three mutually reinforcing sources of constraint truly exists, the proposition that governments with national economies that are more committed to reciprocal trade relations are less inclined to initiate interstate war will be substantiated. To assess the accuracy of this relationship properly, trends in foreign trade are briefly surveyed to underscore the importance of trade to the development of national economies and of international commerce to international relations. In addition, a review of past research on the effects of trade on international politics provides background on relevant indicators of trade and the available sources of data for such measures.

TRADE IN ECONOMIC HISTORY

With the growth of modern economies, foreign trade has assumed a major role in the economic life of most nations; some economic historians even regard it as the principal engine of economic growth. The increased economic efficiencies produced by trade foster capital accumulation to sustain economic expansion (Maizels, 1963). Firms engaged in industrial activity gain as a result of access to larger and more varied markets, and economies that can only export the raw materials used by industrial nations can industrialize through a process of import substitution, whereby their dependence on the manufactured goods of other nations is replaced by domestic industries once markets are created.

Foreign trade may or may not be the most important stimulus to economic growth (Kurth, 1979); what is important, however, is that the economic growth has become a major goal of contemporary societies and that foreign trade is important to prosperity (see Maddison, 1977). Although the demand for greater consumption of goods and services first occurred in the industrial economies of Europe, it has become a general goal for national governments seeking to maintain the approval of their citizens. Whether the principal contributor to growth or not, international commerce satisfies the demand to consume.

This change—the preoccupation of society with growth and the incorporation of trade as a central feature of economic expansion and the meeting of demands for consumption—took place in the global system mainly throughout the nineteenth century:

The dynamic factor underlying the changes that had occurred in world trade by 1914 was the industrialization of western Europe and North America. Western industries such as mass-produced textiles, large-scale metallurgy, power, and steam-driven transport could only play their full role on a world scale; the new increasingly specialized industrial processes of the West had in fact created a productive capacity that could not be absorbed profitably within the confines of any one country. By 1914, encouraged by the increase in the material well-being of many Europeans and the growing commercialization of European life, the consumption of relatively cheap, mass-produced items of commerce was rapidly becoming the goal of western society (Woodruff, 1973, pp. 675–76).

A brief review of developments in the patterns of world trade is necessary in order to understand the political importance of national trade policies and their relation to decisions for war. Perhaps the most notable feature of the development of the global economy—and therefore, of networks of trade—is the stratification of economies according to the timing of industrialization. As one would expect, early-industrializing economies held a dominant position over those that industrialized later and those that have yet to reach a moderate level of industrial wealth (Kuznets, 1968; Organski, 1968), a tendency also reflected by patterns of trade.

As the first region to industrialize, Europe assumed a dominant position in the world economy and its commercial relations. The gains from growth and participation in trade were even more concentrated in Great Britain, the first nation to industrialize and to practice the principles of free trade. The dominance of Britain and Europe in the earlier stage of industrialization is reflected in their proportion of world trade. According to Mulhall (1898, p. 128), in 1750, Great Britain conducted 15 percent of world trade and the rest of Europe 59 percent. By 1889, well into the era of free trade, Britain conducted 22 percent and the rest of Europe 46 percent. These figures demonstrate the Eurocentric nature of the world economy during the early stages of global industrialization. Through the spread of industrial technology as a result of trade, however, other economies could also grow, and thus the general tendency has always been toward the internationalization of the world economy, even though great disparities in wealth remain today.

The first non-European industrial power was the United States, which prospered during the nineteenth century from the benefits of abundant raw materials important to industrial production and the influx of immigrant labor. But even though the United States possessed the largest economy in terms of output in 1914, much larger than any of the economies of Northwest Europe, it traded substantially less than the larger European traders—the result of higher transportation costs and reliance on the North American market, which produced a tendency toward protectionism.

The United States stands out as a rival to the European domination of the world economy. Before the First World War, however, other nations had been launched on a course of modernization through industrialization and world trade. Russia made great industrial strides and was drawn more closely into the European and world economy. Likewise, Japan set out on a course that was to quickly lead it to participate in international economic affairs as a fully industrialized economy.

The first stages of industrialization perhaps led to overoptimism regarding the prospects of other nations' economic expansion. If the European nations, North America, and Japan could industrialize, why should not the other nations of the world also industrialize in time? The failure of the rest of the world economy to industrialize is not a topic that can be addressed here. Nonetheless, the pattern of stratification between industrialized and non-industrialized economies that emerged by the end of the First World War has persisted as an important feature of international economic order. Moreover, such divisions have direct bearing on the interdependence, interpenetration, and interconnection of nations in the global system.

This stratification has had particularly significant implications for patterns of world trade, resulting in a network of trade in which the industrialized economies of Europe exported manufactured goods (55–60 percent of exports) while the economies yet to acquire substantial amounts of industry exported primary products.[1] Interestingly, and as a special case, the United States has traditionally been an exporter of both primary and manufactured goods, as has the Soviet Union depending on the swings of economic policy. This division of world trade bound the pre-industrial nations to the economic performance of European economies and suppressed intraregional trade:

In sharp contrast to the relations that existed earlier between the manufacturing and the primary producing parts of the world, the world's major exporters of manufactured goods were becoming increasingly the world's major importers of manufactured goods. Yet there was no similar tendency on the part of the primary producers of the world to become the leading importers of primary produce. Indeed, for the primary producing countries of the world exactly the opposite situation prevailed. Many countries in Africa, Latin America,

1. See Bairoch, *Commerce extérieur et développement économique de l'Europe au XIXe siècle*, table 27, p. 92. Professor Bairoch informs me that European imports of raw materials were not for industry: "This is a general fallacy, even among economic historians, that already in the 19th century, the developed countries depended on the Third World for a high share of their raw materials. According to recent research (mostly at the University of Geneva) the share of imported raw material for industry represented around 5–10% of the consumption of those goods around 1913 as well as 1937" (personal correspondence to the author, December 1980).

Asia, and Australia—many of them part of Europe's colonial empires—had become so accustomed to meeting the demands of a particular European country, sometimes the demands of a particular European industry, that by 1913 they were unable (especially those who through intense international specialization had become committed to a system of monoculture) to deal with anybody else, least of all their immediate neighbors (Woodruff, 1973, p. 686).

Because the many independent Latin American governments are included in analyses of decisions for war, the status of the Latin American economies is of particular importance. (Most other exporters of primary products were still part of a colonial empire during the nineteenth century.) Although the content of Latin American trade was different from European trade, given the lower level of industrial development, it was substantial in terms of national incomes. Including Latin American economies in analyses of the nineteenth century thus allows us to compare the effects of various levels of trade on governments of economies in both the manufacturing and primary-product-exporting regions.

One important aspect of international commerce in a global economy marked by great disparity deserves special mention, for although it plays no direct part in the analyses that follow, it strongly determines levels of trade, that is, exports and imports as a share of total economic output. The level of trade between the primary-goods exporters and their industrialized consumers is affected by the terms of trade between economies, that is, by the ratio of relative prices of imported versus exported goods. Although there is some disagreement among economic historians, it seems most likely that the growth of trade in primary products benefited from increasingly favorable terms of trade until the economically unstable 1930s and the protectionist policies that ensued. Since then, the terms of trade for pre-industrial economies exporting raw materials has worsened (Bairoch, 1975, chap. 6). Because exporters of primary products have had more difficulty maintaining levels of trade since the 1930s, they should, given the theoretical arguments of chapter 2, be more prone to wage war.

Before examining research on trade in international politics, it is useful to survey briefly the history of international commerce since 1815 in order to demonstrate the dynamic pace of global economic change and its likely effects on decisions for war. With the end of the Napoleonic Wars, Europe and the world economy gained the tranquility necessary for trade to prosper, and the free-trade ethic flowered in these early years of the nineteenth century. Even so, trade did not expand rapidly until a period of parliamentary reform permitted the passage of the Free Trade Acts of 1846, which greatly reduced British customs duties (see Kindleberger, 1978).

The greatest sustained expansion of world trade in modern times ensued. Measured in constant prices, world trade expanded four-fold by 1879 (Kuznets, 1966, table 6.3, p. 306). While the British held the largest share of international commerce, the other nations of Europe soon followed in expanding their trade activities. By 1860, the primary-goods exporters of Asia and Latin America also began to enlarge their foreign-trade capacities, and in the fifty years before the First World War, their exports grew at a much faster rate than did the Europeans'.

Germany's imposition of protectionist policies interrupted the first period of free trade in 1879. In fact, all developed countries except for Great Britain and the Netherlands erected trade barriers in the period 1879–92. This led to a decade of much slower trade growth, but was later replaced by rapid growth, which continued until the First World War. Protectionist trade barriers were erected by only a few European governments, and most other trading nations managed to adapt their economies to the new conditions (Kindleberger, 1978). The limited number of governments restricting imports meant that growth in trade was soon resumed, and exports from primary-goods producers grew the most during this period.

The start of the First World War in 1914 marks the beginning of what some economic historians call the Great Depression of 1914 through 1945. It is well documented that war and economic instability reduce foreign trade far more than they curtail economic growth (see Kuznets, 1966, pp. 317–21); this is consistent with the theoretical argument that posits the pacifistic interests of business elites involved in trade. Although the 1920s were years of relative economic prosperity, foreign trade had barely caught up with pre-war levels when the economic instabilities of the 1930s reduced trade prospects once more (see Pollard, 1981, chap. 8).

The decline of trade in the interwar period was also encouraged by the autarkic policies of several formerly large trading nations. The Soviet Union chose a more self-reliant strategy of economic growth, and there was difficulty in making trade agreements between centrally planned and free-market economies. Germany, after 1933, reduced its exports as a strategy of increasing influence over Eastern European governments (see Hirschman, 1945). The combined reduction of Soviet and German exports naturally affected their smaller traditional trading partners, which also experienced more dramatic curtailments of exports than would be expected solely in terms of restricted markets produced by worldwide depression. This had obvious implications for the incidence of war and testifies directly to the close relationship of foreign trade activity and decision for war.

The post–World War II era saw the resumption of growth in world trade. It was encouraged by the U.S. government which, as the leader of the world's largest economy and one left intact by the war, was in a position to guide postwar trade policies (Milward, 1979, chap. 10). The free-trade ethic has existed (although only as a rival to protectionist tariffs) in U.S. domestic and foreign policy since colonial times (see Keohane, 1983), and as the dominant position of the postwar period, it provided an opportunity to build an international structure of free trade (see Maier, 1977). U.S. policy reflected the belief that high levels of foreign trade and international economic interdependence were vital to the achievement of prosperity and political stability that was necessary for peace, an inclination that was manifestly reinforced by the lessons of the 1930s, when the rapid spread of trade restrictions encouraged economic nationalism as an elemental cause of World War II.

To manage international commerce, new global institutions were created to facilitate transfers of goods. Not only did the United Nations act to encourage trade, but new institutions such as the International Bank for Reconstruction and Development, the International Monetary Fund, the General Agreement on Tariffs and Trade, and the Organization for Economic Cooperation and Development have played major roles in regulating and stimulating world trade. Soon, too, attempts at regional economic integration took place with mixed success. Economic integration in Europe has greatly facilitated trade between economies, but Latin American and African experiments have not led to rising trade.

The environment of free trade, which has led to generally low tariff levels, has helped sustain high rates of economic growth. Almost every national economy has grown greatly, but the world economy continues to be stratified between richer industrial nations and poorer nations with little industrial capacity.

The history of trade in the world economy can be divided into three periods (see also Maddison, 1977). The nineteenth century marks the incorporation of the free-trade ethic into the actions of governments and practices of business elites pursuing foreign markets. The period as a whole saw tremendous increases in levels of trade, even if somewhat interrupted by a wave of protectionism in the 1880s.

The years between the First and Second World Wars constitute a separate period framed by the disruption of trade by the First World War and the drastic reductions of trade produced by the Depression and national governments pursuing autarkic policies. No other period in the history of the world economy has been marked by such great economic dislocation and reversals in patterns of growth.

The years following the Second World War witnessed the resumption of economic expansion and the enlargement of international trade. The structural characteristics of this period were developed to ensure that only the most severe economic disruption—such as world war or massive resource scarcity—could interrupt international commerce in the way it was interrupted in the interwar years.

The review of commercial history is important to the ability to judge correctly whether the source of foreign-trade constraint stems from interdependence, interpenetration, or interconnection. The complementary nature of these sources of constraint, however, makes it difficult to create firm hypotheses. Nonetheless, three tentative hypothetical expectations can be offered. First, it is a reasonable assumption that the most vulnerable economies are those preindustrial or Third World economies reliant on the export of primary products. If these governments go to war, then interdependence does not seem to constrain. Second, the constraint of interconnection is based on the growing specialization of national economies. This dynamic consequence of foreign trade suggests that constraints will build over time; in other words, trading nations may go to war in earlier times, but over time war will become rarer. Third, if interpenetration is the source of constraint, then governments of trading nations would be less inclined to decide for war in any period and without regard to the nature of export commodities. This pattern might be distorted, however, in periods of global economic depression when foreign trade is disrupted by widespread protectionist measures to stimulate national economic growth.

TRADE AND INTERNATIONAL POLITICS

Despite its relevance to global political interaction, the study of international commerce has occupied a variable position in the literature of world politics. In the aftermath of World War I, the study of international relations tended to center on legal and economic interactions at the expense of power politics. To many, the outcome of the Great War altered the traditional foundations of international relations and suggested a need for greater study of economic interaction and international organization (see Carr, 1939 chap. 3). The outcome of the Second World War suggested just the opposite, and notions of power politics dominated the field. However, by the late 1960s, attention returned to economic interactions, foreign trade, and their role in world politics (for example, Cooper, 1968). Studies of foreign trade can be grouped according to two general orientations. Many studies emphasize the importance of transnational relations represented by foreign trade; others focus on the importance of government in promoting the economic position of the nation.

Research in the area of the first category revolves around transnationalism as a trend in international politics. Of particular importance are the works of Karl Deutsch, whose interest focuses on foreign trade as an important ingredient in the establishment of reciprocal bonds between national societies. A study published in 1961 investigated long-term trends in the proportion of national income involved in trade and concluded that declining trade shares left little hope for future international collaboration (Deutsch and Eckstein, 1961). Deutsch's conclusion that exports as a percentage of national income had declined in industrially advanced economies was later contradicted by the work of Kuznets (1966; see also Aldcroft, 1981, pp. 306–07), but it led to further interest in the relationships of trade partners to economic integration (see Russett, 1967).

The second and growing area of research focuses on the activities of the government in regulating foreign trade through economic policy. The connection between government and trade was clearly depicted in Hirschman's (1945) investigation of the trade policies of Nazi Germany and their effect on the world economy and the national economies with which it traditionally traded. Similarly, a "statist" approach to the study of international economic relations recognizes the activities of national governments, which as the most powerful actor in a polity are central to the understanding of trade policies (Krasner, 1978; Gilpin, 1975).

The degree of trade interdependence and its implications for the structure of the global system generated a debate in the literature (the major contributions are collected in Maghoori and Ramberg, 1982). To scholars of the power-politics school, interdependence modifies relations only if it constrains the actions of great powers (Waltz, 1970). Since the two superpowers of the post–World War II era trade much less than great powers of the past, a case can be made that there is less interdependence in the contemporary epoch (Waltz, 1979, chap. 7). Using a variety of indicators associated with economic interactions, others have concluded that interdependence has varied a great deal over time, but has reached a high level since 1945 (Rosecrance and Stein, 1973; Rosecrance et al., 1977). Still others note how trade relationships are built into a global system characterized by "complex interdependence," which supports nongovernmental actors and constrains the use of force (Keohane and Nye, 1977).

Systematic research about the relationship of foreign trade to war is lacking, however, despite the many arguments advanced earlier about its role in decisions for war. The theoretical arguments concerning the importance of trade to war have not been met by empirical research designed to ascertain the existence of any relationships. Many arguments have been advanced about the correlation of economic structures and war without any empirical support (for example, Buzan, 1984). Two recent research efforts stand out as exceptions. Using trade and conflict data for thirty nations for the period 1958–63, Sol Polachek found that on a dyadic level, the more two nations trade together, the less the conflictual behavior between them (1980). Mark Gasiorowski also found that trade volume was inversely related to conflict (1986). Using a variety of variables for 130 nations between 1948 and 1977, he further found that other forms of economic interaction were positively related to conflictual behaviors.

CONSTRUCTING INDICATORS OF TRADE ACTIVITY

The absence of cross-temporally and cross-nationally comparable indicators of foreign trade does not reflect a lack of interest in trade phenomena on the part of economic historians, merely the difficulty with which data can be gathered and made comparable (see Maizels, 1963; Kuznets, 1966; Bairoch, 1976). But fortunately, the data and examples of methods of procedure to create comparable measures are available. Because the hypothesis advanced here—that foreign trade produces a constraint on decisions for war through the growth of international, domestic, and governmental forces with a stake in open and unfettered foreign dealings—the relevant indicator of foreign trade would measure an economy's involvement in trade. If trade is related negatively to decisions for war, then comparisons with an indicator of trade involvement will reflect such a relationship. For the hypothesis here, this is superior to other indicators and research designs. An alternative indicator used in research on integration is a measure of trade-partner concentration of exports. The hypothesis that trade constrains decisions for war is not dyadic, but national in focus. Besides, dyadic indicators would not reflect the importance of foreign trade in a nation's economy, only the importance of individual trading partners in foreign trade. It is the cumulative or most extensive role of commercial interests that is relevant here. Dyadic indicators would tap more narrow and specialized interests within the foreign-trading sector of the economy, which would also be misleading. For example, in the years before the Balkan Wars, one-third of Bulgarian exports went to Turkey, reflecting their common border and Bulgaria's lack of outside ports (*Statesman's Yearbook*, 1911, p. 675). As we shall see, however, at the same time, Bulgaria was the world's smallest trader, when measured by exports as a share of GNP. It is the small size of the export sector that is important, not the distribution of trading partners.

The appropriate indicator is exports as a proportion of national income or some other measure of gross national economic output. The alternative—the level of imports—is a quite different aspect of foreign trade and inappropriate for three reasons. First, its relation to economic growth is indirect, as very few domestic businesses benefit from importing because no new production is stimulated. In fact, economic expansion is often stifled through dependence on foreign products. Second, business elites engaged in import trade would not develop the same interest in foreign markets as the much more numerous elites generating export trade. Finally, governments usually organize to promote exports and *limit* imports as a means to improve a nation's balance-of-payments position.

This is not to say that imports may not have a bearing on decisions for war. Since levels of imports generally relate to the availability of goods that compete with domestic production, if foreign trade appears to hurt domestic industrial interests, even those who conduct an export trade may come to favor protectionist policies that would then tend to remove what constraint on war might exist. This depends not on the level of export or import trade, but on the relation of the two and, perhaps more importantly, the effects of foreign competition in selected sectors of the economy. To include the consideration of import activity would thus greatly complicate the analyses conducted here.

Also, imports may provide various consumer goods or, at least, some goods at lower prices. It may be, therefore, that mass publics of economies that import a great deal of consumer goods would favor cooperative foreign policies in order to protect their supply of such goods. To answer such a question, not only would data on imports be required, but they would need to be separated according to the quantity of imports of various types of goods. Because of this difficulty, as well as the ones noted above, imports will not be included in the analyses here.

The desired indicator—export trade as a percentage of national income—is a simple measure to construct. The data required, however, are not always readily available. On the one hand, governments have for centuries gathered trade statistics for the purpose of collecting customs revenue. On the other hand, though, measures of national income have become reliably available only since the Second World War, when the concept of GNP became widely accepted and estimated. Therefore, the data on national income for earlier periods are far less reliable, especially for smaller non-European economies. Because of these limitations, no analyses can be reasonably conducted before 1870, when a good portion of the independent governments were small German or Italian states and estimates of total product are extremely rare and unreliable.

The final measure used here is composed of the ratio of two indicators: exports and total output. Perhaps the most troublesome aspect of comparing the two figures is that export trade is usually reported in current currency, which does not reflect movement in prices, while estimates of total output performed by economic historians are almost always in constant currency (or an index) reflecting their interest in studying patterns of growth unaffected by changes in prices. This is not a problem for the period between 1948 and 1975 because data have been made available by the United Nations, which has standardized the procedures of national income accounting and published relevant data. For this period, data are taken from economic statistics compiled by the World Bank and made available on magnetic tape. In these compilations, data for both exports and GNP are shown in both current and constant currencies, making the construction of a percentage figure straightforward. For nations for which data are not available from the World Bank (centrally planned economies and for all nations in the years 1948 and 1949), data are taken from various annual editions of the U.N. *Yearbook of Trade Statistics and Yearbook of National Accounts Statistics.* The U.S. Central Intelligence Agency's *Handbook of Economic Statistics* was consulted as a check on the procedures and supplement for centrally planned economies.

The information-gathering of the United Nations was preceded by the League of Nations. For the period 1913–39, trade statistics have been published for all but a few independent governments (Iran, Liberia, Ethiopia, Saudi Arabia, and Yemen).[2] These statistics are only available in current prices, however. Because an export price index is not available for each nation concerned, a single one must be used. This practice is consistent with a previous study engaged in cross-national comparison of trade during the interwar period:

In reality the prices of manufactured articles imported or exported by different countries do not, of course, follow the same course; it can be shown, for instance, that a relative expansion of a country's export of manufactured articles is usually accompanied by a relative decline in its export prices. . . . Moreover, in the present study we are less concerned with changes in the quantum of trade proper than with the variations in the inflow and outflow of foreign currency that such changes reflect. The use of a common price index for different prices is thus justified and may even be advantageous, since the various "values at 1913 prices" for each period then maintain the same mutual relationship as the actual values (Hilgerdt, 1945, p. 156).

The price indices used in the League of Nations study are used here. Two indices are available for the period divided into several subperiods (1920, 1921–25, 1926–29, 1930, 1931–35, 1936–39), representing averages of years whose trade patterns are most similar. The analyses conducted for the interwar years will therefore be with exports as a percent of GNP averaged across each period and deflated according to the relevant price index.

Twelve nations identified as exporting primarily manufactured goods (Austria, Belgium, Czechoslovakia, France, Germany, Italy, Japan, the Netherlands, Sweden, Switzerland, United Kingdom, and the United States) are deflated with an index of prices of world

2. League of Nations, Economic and Financial Section, *International Statistical Yearbook 1926* (Geneva: League of Nations, 1927), pp. 108–11; League of Nations, Economic Intelligence Service, *Statistical Yearbook 1933/34* (Geneva: League of Nations, 1934), pp. 187–90; League of Nations, Economic Intelligence Service, *Statistical Yearbook 1940/44* (Geneva: League of Nations, 1941), pp. 167–72.

exports in manufactured goods. All others are made constant with the use of a price index for exports in primary goods (agriculture, mining, and "light" processing of raw materials) (Hilgerdt, 1945 p. 152).

Estimates of GNP for this period are less readily available, as they are based on the calculations by economic historians using information known to be related to national income and economic output. Estimates of GNP have been acquired in two ways using data from three sources. Folke Hilgerdt provides indices of production of manufactured goods for the twenty-nine most industrial economies (1945, table 1, pp. 130–31). These indices based on industrial activity can be used to extend a series of total output for each of these economies if it is assumed that production of primary goods does not radically differ from that of industrial production. In most industrial economies, this assumption is fairly sound because the production of primary goods is closely tied to their consumption by industry within the economy.

A GNP series can be constructed from a common base year of GNP. The year 1929 marks the greatest recovery of the world economy after the First World War and the last before the disruption of the 1930s. Paul Bairoch provides estimates of GNP for each European economy in the territorial units of the time for the year 1929.[3] These figures can then be extended with the use of Hilgerdt's index of industrial production. Maizels reports comparable GNP estimates for non-European industrial nations (the United States, Japan, Australia, and New Zealand) that can also be extended over the entire period (Maizels, 1963, p. 531).

The quality of these figures is quite high and reflects the interest of economic historians in the long-term growth of industrial nations. Far less work has been done on the non-industrial economies of the Third World. One group of estimates appears reliable and can be used to estimate GNP for the remaining independent nations in the global system. By estimating the size of a country's pop-

3. Bairoch, "Europe's Gross National Product, 1800–1975," table 10, p. 295. An aggregate figure is provided for the three Baltic states, which is divided according to the size of their respective populations in 1929 (Estonia, 1.1 million; Latvia, 1.8 million; and Lithuania, 2.3 million). It is a fairly safe assumption that the per capita incomes of these nations were very similar.

ulation and then its per capita income, L. J. Zimmerman was able to estimate the national income of non-European economies (Zimmerman, 1962). While there is no real method with which to check these estimates, they are intuitively valid and have been used by several economic historians who accept Zimmerman's work.[4]

Because no annualized index of output is available, these estimates can only be extrapolated over the period of interest. Zimmerman (1962) provides estimates of national income for 1913, 1929, and 1952. If the assumption is that the pre-industrial economies which did not participate in the First World War were less affected by it, except for their foreign trade, then the extrapolation between points is not perhaps a too significant misrepresentation of true national incomes (see Aldcroft, 1981, pp. 39–41; Hardach, 1977, chap. 9). Whatever the case, they are perhaps the only estimates available and must certainly reflect the relative size of national economies in this period, even if with some error. This is perhaps inadequate for the economic historian, who wishes to chart economic conditions carefully, but fully acceptable for this study, which requires systematically comparable data on the relative size of output across nations.

Zimmerman could not provide estimates for Liberia, Ethiopia, or the several independent Middle Eastern nations. Indeed, even the population of these countries at the time is unknown. While some trade data are available from the League of Nations, it does not seem reasonable to guess at a figure of national income for these economies, and they are, as a consequence, omitted from this analysis.

These same procedures were used to estimate national incomes for the period prior to the First World War. Ten-year estimates of GNP for industrial nations were extrapolated to create estimates for

4. See the most recent treatment in Aldcroft (1981, chap. 12). Paul Bairoch, however, notes that Zimmerman's estimates are on the whole, quite reliable, but that several assumptions lead, on balance, to the overestimation of output growth in Latin America and underestimation of growth in Asia. However, no better estimates exist for the national economies of these nations in the nineteenth century. See Paul Bairoch, "Le Volume des Productions et du Produit National dans le Tiers Monde (1900–1977)," *Revue Tiers Monde* 20 (October, 1979). The methodological appendix supplied by Bairoch is especially valuable.

five-year periods beginning in 1871 and ending with a short period of 1911–13 (Bairoch, 1976, table 6, p. 286). All other nations, principally Latin American, were extrapolated based on Zimmerman's estimates for 1860, 1880, 1900, and 1913. Unlike the interwar period, this era was characterized by steady rates of growth, and it is less likely that linear extrapolation of these points would gloss over radical changes in national incomes that might otherwise be missed. Cyclical movements more often occurred in industrial economies for which Bairoch's data is more sound. The five-year averages would also tend to correct for divergencies from a linear trend.

Export statistics for this period do not exist in comparable form, for no international organization was available to compile them. This is particularly true for the Third World producers of primary goods, again reflecting the greater interest of economic historians in the industrially advanced economies. One study compiled the necessary export statistics for the years 1860, 1880, and 1900 (Hanson, 1980) in a manner amenable for the comparison with Zimmerman's estimates of national income, making them useful for this study. Although they are displayed in current currency, after extrapolating the figures for all nations between the years given (and 1913 provided by the League of Nations), they are deflated with the two price series for five-year periods provided back to 1870 in Hilgerdt (1945).

The two variables used to construct the indicator of export activity were compiled with an eye toward comparability across nations as well as time. Instead of treating the indicator of trade used here as accurate percentages of national income derived from the export of goods and services, it is perhaps best to think of it as an index of levels of exports that can be used to compare activity across time and nations.

The limitations of this data cannot be overemphasized. Whereas the data for the period since 1948 are sound, the indices for the earlier periods were constructed with an eye toward comparability and not historical detail. Major improvements could be made for the non-European economies in the nineteenth century. In particular, more specialized commodity-price indices could be used to deflate trade data. The use of the single price index for primary products overlooks variation in price movements across numerous commodities. Since the analyses presented below show strong relationships, further analyses should be attentive to the work of economic historians.[5] The results of the procedures described above for the United Kingdom, France, Germany, and the United States are quite close to those reported by Kuznets, who constructed a similar measure using time-series particular to each economy (Kuznets, 1967). The other figures cannot be so compared, but they are consistent with what was anticipated given knowledge of trends in foreign trade.

FOREIGN TRADE AND DECISIONS FOR WAR

A first set of analyses can be conducted on the index of export activity derived from the procedures described above. This is the simplest and most obvious relationship to be examined. Since the occurrence of war upsets trade patterns, comparisons must be made for the year prior to the outbreak of war to avoid the possibility that war's effect on trade will bias comparisons. The data for the interwar years pose some limitations. No data are available for 1919, and therefore 1920 is used for the comparisons of the wars beginning in 1919. Similarly, the analysis for 1920 is not based on the previous year. Finally, because the necessary data does not exist for Ethiopia in 1935, only Italy is contrasted with the other independent governments in the system for which data is available.

A second analysis can be done for *changes* in exports as a percentage of GNP prior to the outbreak of war. Are governments for which the share of national income going to exports is declining or growing slowly more likely to wage war than nations with an expanding trade sector? This question can be examined by calculating for each nation the percentage change in exports as a percentage of GNP from the previous five-year period, recalling that from 1871 to 1938 data exist only averaged over subperiods. For the period from 1949 to 1975, data are averaged for five years before war to make

5. Major improvements are necessary for the nineteenth century, where Zimmerman's GNP data need improvement. Better price series are also needed, especially ones that can be tied to the commodities being traded. Improved accuracy introduces considerable complexity that is beyond the scope of this study. Of course, none of these problems exist for the data since 1948.

comparisons comparable to earlier periods. For the four war years that occur in the first five years after the conclusion to the two world wars, no analysis can be made.

One further analysis is necessary. Exports as a share of national income vary according to the size of the economy (Kuznets, 1966; Taagepera, 1976). Larger economies tend to trade less because the size of the domestic market provides considerable demand to stimulate growth, whereas smaller economies must seek foreign markets in order to stimulate production and maintain economic growth (see table 5.1).

Also, the major powers in international politics possess the largest economies (that, indeed, is part of what makes them more "powerful"). In addition, these major powers have participated in more wars in this period than their smaller counterparts. One would, therefore, expect to find a negative relationship between exports as a percentage of GNP and decisions for war.

Such a situation can be controlled for, however. An ordinary least squares regression of exports/GNP on GNP in constant dollars will yield a predicted relationship, the deviations from which can be analyzed. These "residual" percentages would be the divergence for each nation/year from what would be expected, given the size of the economy as measured by GNP. Comparisons could then be made as before, except that instead of comparing percentages themselves, differences from the tendency of large nations to trade less are examined. In this way, the tendency of larger nations with smaller export ratios to go to war will be accounted for.

This control for size was accomplished by first computing the natural log of GNP in constant currency to produce a linear relationship with exports as a percentage of GNP. An ordinary least squares regression could then be performed for each period and the "residual" export percentages used in analysis. The relationship between logged GNP and exports as a percentage of GNP is strongest in the pre–World War I period (slope $= -4.87$, $r^2 = .20$) and quite similar for the later two periods (interwar: slope $= -2.26$, $r^2 = .08$; post–World War II: slope $= -2.19$, $r^2 = .05$). Each estimation produced statistically significant coefficients, and a curvilinear fit of the two variables yielded only an extremely small improvement on the merely linear model for each period.

126

TABLE 5.1   EXPORTS AS A SHARE OF NATIONAL OUTPUT (SELECTED
YEARS: 1913, 1938, 1964)

1913

Nation	Index 1ª	Index 2ᵇ	Nationᶜ	Index 1	Index 2
Cuba	100.0	91.9	Norway	15.8	−2.6
Bolivia	82.3	63.8	Ecuador	15.5	−16.5
Netherlands	75.9	74.2	GERMANY	13.9	11.2
Uruguay	54.0	35.3	Colombia	13.4	−10.3
Nicaragua	49.3	19.1	Venezuela	11.8	−12.1
BELGIUM	43.5	37.0	El Salvador	10.8	−22.1
FRANCE	29.9	27.4	AUSTRIA-HUNGARY	8.7	3.4
Peru	29.2	5.5	Romania	8.1	−10.5
Haiti	26.7	−2.8	Paraguay	7.8	−27.1
Brazil	26.1	13.2	RUSSIA	7.2	3.4
Italy	24.8	18.6	Chile	6.8	−12.9
Guatemala	22.7	−5.7	United States	6.7	6.4
Argentina	21.2	6.6	Spain	6.1	−7.5
Switzerland	21.0	7.0	Honduras	5.2	−30.5
Denmark	20.2	4.1	China	3.0	−4.7
Mexico	19.0	1.8	Turkey	2.9	−15.7
UNITED KINGDOM	18.4	16.1	Greece	2.9	−19.1
Thailand	17.6	−4.4	SERBIA	2.8	−22.7
Sweden	16.4	1.6	Portugal	2.6	−18.6
Dominican Rep.	16.2	−13.6	Bulgaria	.9	−23.2
JAPAN	16.0	2.8	Ethiopia	missing data	
			Persia	missing data	

1938

Ireland	100.0	12.7	FINLAND	49.6	−0.3
Haiti	92.0	7.1	CANADA	48.7	2.8
Peru	81.1	6.9	Estonia	45.3	−4.9
NEW ZEALAND	80.2	8.3	AUSTRALIA	43.7	0.8
SOUTH AFRICA	70.6	7.1	Switzerland	41.2	−2.2
Japan	64.4	8.3	Sweden	37.2	−1.5
Cuba	58.4	1.3	Mexico	37.0	−2.3
Argentina	57.1	4.4	Norway	35.0	−3.9
Denmark	56.7	2.8	Ecuador	34.0	−8.8
Belgium	53.7	3.0	Bolivia	31.9	−9.9
Uruguay	53.4	−1.5	Netherlands	31.6	−3.1

ªIndex 1 = Exports as a share of GNP expressed in relation to the largest trading nation.
ᵇIndex 2 = Exports as a share of GNP controlling for size. Figures show the deviation
    from the expected value, derived from a regression of Index 1 on GNP.
ᶜNations shown in capitals decided for war in the subsequent year.

Continued on next page

Table 5.1 *Continued*

Nation	Index 1[a]	Index 2[b]	Nation[c]	Index 1	Index 2
Thailand	31.3	−6.8	FRANCE	17.8	−4.0
Nicaragua	31.2	−13.3	Costa Rica	16.2	−17.6
Colombia	31.1	−5.6	GERMANY	14.9	−3.7
UNITED KINGDOM	31.1	1.1	China	14.7	−5.1
Brazil	31.0	−2.4	Italy	14.5	−6.1
El Salvador	31.0	−10.8	POLAND	11.3	−8.7
Bulgaria	26.5	−8.6	Honduras	11.2	−17.5
Panama	26.0	−13.2	United States	10.9	−2.3
Dominican Rep.	25.8	−11.7	Portugal	5.2	−11.5
Venezuela	25.8	−7.3	SOVIET UNION	.8	−8.5
Paraguay	25.8	−7.3	Afghanistan	missing data	
Czechoslovakia	25.5	−13.4	Albania	missing data	
Chile	23.9	−8.3	Egypt	missing data	
Turkey	23.4	−6.1	Iran	missing data	
Greece	23.4	−7.6	Iraq	missing data	
Guatemala	23.2	−12.0	Liberia	missing data	
Hungary	21.8	−7.5	Luxemburg	missing data	
Latvia	20.4	−9.5	Mongolia	missing data	
Yugoslavia	20.0	−8.8	Nepal	missing data	
Lithuania	19.2	−11.1	Saudi Arabia	missing data	
Romania	18.4	−7.1	Spain	missing data	
			Yemen	missing data	
1964					
Singapore	100.0	65.3	Malta	55.4	20.4
Kuwait	95.3	64.1	Malaysia	52.6	24.4
Luxemburg	89.3	55.1	Trinidad	50.4	19.6
Saudi Arabia	85.2	54.1	Netherlands	49.5	26.7
Zaire	79.0	46.8	Iraq	48.5	21.1
Libya	76.3	45.7	Gambia	45.6	8.2
Liberia	73.5	37.2	Norway	45.1	20.3
Zambia	68.6	37.0	Jamaica	44.8	14.7
Gabon	63.7	29.3	Iceland	43.2	12.3
Congo	58.5	23.7	Panama	41.4	11.0
Mauritania	55.8	20.7	Belgium	40.1	17.6

[a]Index 1 = Exports as a share of GNP expressed in relation to the largest trading nation.

[b]Index 2 = Exports as a share of GNP controlling for size. Figures show the deviation from the expected value, derived from a regression of Index 1 on GNP.

[c]Nations shown in capitals decided for war in the subsequent year.

Table 5.1 *Continued*

Nation	Index 1[a]	Index 2[b]	Nation[c]	Index 1	Index 2
Lebanon	39.4	10.1	Bulgaria	20.7	−2.7
Venezuela	38.1	14.2	Taiwan	20.4	−4.1
Kenya	37.9	8.7	United Kingdom	20.4	3.3
Ireland	37.1	10.8	Thailand	20.3	−3.8
Ivory Coast	36.9	7.9	Cameroun	20.3	−7.7
Nicaragua	34.5	4.6	Peru	20.3	−3.7
Sierra Leone	34.3	2.7	Nigeria	20.1	−3.3
Denmark	33.9	11.1	Ecuador	19.9	−7.1
Switzerland	33.5	11.6	Philippines	19.7	−3.9
Cyprus	33.5	2.8	Egypt	19.6	−4.0
Central African R.	31.3	−1.0	Ghana	19.3	−6.8
Somalia	31.0	−1.8	Honduras	19.2	−6.5
South Africa	30.7	7.9	Guatemala	19.2	−7.6
El Salvador	29.7	0.7	Guinea	18.8	−10.7
Tanzania	29.3	0.8	Italy	18.6	0.7
Sri Lanka	29.0	0.6	Sudan	18.6	−7.7
Austria	27.8	5.4	Dahomey	18.2	−12.6
Portugal	27.8	3.5	Malagasy	18.2	−9.7
Uganda	27.6	−0.7	Poland	17.8	−1.5
Chad	26.6	−4.3	Uruguay	17.8	−7.7
Costa Rica	25.9	−3.1	Jordan	17.5	−10.6
Senegal	25.9	−2.1	Australia	17.2	−2.4
Algeria	25.7	0.8	Dominican Rep.	16.8	−10.4
Iran	24.6	1.6	Paraguay	16.7	−11.7
Sweden	24.4	4.1	Burma	16.1	−9.9
New Zealand	24.4	0.7	Chile	15.9	−6.8
Yugoslavia	24.2	1.5	France	15.2	−1.2
Finland	23.7	.8	Niger	15.2	−13.5
Bolivia	23.1	−5.6	Mali	15.0	−15.0
Togo	22.9	−8.3	German D.R.	14.4	−4.8
Morocco	22.7	−2.6	Haiti	14.3	−14.6
Syria	22.3	−4.6	Rwanda	13.5	−17.5
Canada	21.7	3.2	Ethiopia	13.3	−12.8
Tunisia	21.4	−5.6	Colombia	12.9	−10.3
Israel	21.3	−3.3	Cambodia	12.8	−15.8
F.R. Germany	21.1	5.1	Spain	12.3	−7.0
Malawi	20.9	−9.6	Japan	12.0	−3.8

[a]Index 1 = Exports as a share of GNP expressed in relation to the largest trading nation.
[b]Index 2 = Exports as a share of GNP controlling for size. Figures show the deviation from the expected value, derived from a regression of Index 1 on GNP.
[c]Nations shown in capitals decided for war in the subsequent year.

Continued on next page

Table 5.1 *Continued*

Nation	Index 1[a]	Index 2[b]	Nation[c]	Index 1	Index 2
Burundi	11.6	−18.8	Albania	6.1	−21.6
Mexico	10.9	−8.7	Indonesia	5.9	−15.6
Greece	10.0	−12.1	UNITED STATES	5.4	−6.0
Afghanistan	9.9	−16.7	INDIA	4.4	−13.2
South Korea	9.4	−13.6	North Korea	2.7	−20.9
PAKISTAN	9.4	−13.8	Soviet Union	2.4	−10.9
Romania	9.4	−11.4	P.R. China	2.2	−13.2
Hungary	9.3	−11.6	NORTH VIETNAM	1.7	−22.6
Czechoslovakia	9.2	−9.9	Cuba	missing data	
Upper Volta	9.1	−19.7	Laos	missing data	
SOUTH VIETNAM	9.1	−15.4	Maldive Islands	missing data	
Argentina	8.6	−10.8	Mongolia	missing data	
Brazil	8.3	−10.4	Nepal	missing data	
Turkey	6.9	−14.0	Yemen A.R.	missing data	

[a]Index 1 = Exports as a share of GNP expressed in relation to the largest trading nation.
[b]Index 2 = Exports as a share of GNP controlling for size. Figures show the deviation from the expected value, derived from a regression of Index 1 on GNP.
[c]Nations shown in capitals decided for war in the subsequent year.

The appropriate statistical technique with which to make the comparisons called for by the hypothesis is determined by the two variables being examined. A dichotomous outcome is predicted by a continuous variable. This restricts analysis to the use of a probit model which transforms the outcome variable according to its distribution in order to calculate probabilities of predicting various outcomes with the continuous explanatory variables (Finney, 1971; Hanuskek and Jackson, 1977, chap. 14). The technique is analogous to modeling relationships with regression equations and differs only in the ability to evaluate models whose coefficients are restricted by the dichotomous nature of the outcome phenomenon. Because the probit model iteratively searches for the best prediction of the outcome phenomenon, results can be thought of in terms of probabilities or the likelihood that a given outcome is correctly predicted on the basis of the explanatory variable.

The results of analysis for each of the three variables discussed above are shown in table 5.2. The coefficient for each year in which a war occurs is a slope showing the change in a transformed outcome variable given a unit change in the explanatory variable. In other words, a positive coefficient in these analyses indicates that higher export percentages are related to decisions for war and negative relationships fit the hypothesis that decisions for war are associated with lower exports as a percentage of national income. Because the coefficient measures change in a transformed outcome variable, their interpretation is limited to the strength and direction of any relationship and not to unit changes in the dichotomous outcome. The level of significance reports the probability that the coefficient was arrived at by chance. A low probability reflects a greater certainty in the relationship described by the coefficient.

The coefficients and their statistical significance reported in table 5.2 strongly support the hypothesis: governments of economies that export less are more likely to make decisions for war. For exports as a percentage of GNP, twenty-three of thirty-one (74%) war years are in the hypothesized negative relationship. The significance levels vary, of course, but eleven years meet a criterion of 95 percent certainty in the relationship discerned.

The war years in the period from 1871 to 1914 are consistently negative (71%). Interestingly, for the four years in which the relationship is in the opposite direction as hypothesized, the wars being analyzed were waged by Latin American nations (the Pacific War of 1879 and the three Central American wars of 1885, 1906, and 1907). It has already been noted that Latin American exporters of primary products became large traders in this period, and in waging wars against each other, it should come as no surprise that positive relationships result. Bolivia, in fact, had many concessions to foreign firms to export minerals. In 1879, at the time of war with Chile, Bolivia was the world's most extensive trader, if measured as exports as a percent of GNP. The Bolivian government canceled contracts to Chilean firms as a way to gain more domestic control, and this act prompted the Chilean invasion. The case can be made that Latin American nations were not integrated into the world economy in the same manner as the other, more industrialized nations because domestic exporters were secondary to foreign firms exporting primary products. This is an important finding, somewhat tempered by the lower confidence in data for this region in

131

TABLE 5.2   FOREIGN TRADE AND DECISIONS FOR WAR

Year	Exports/GNP		% Change of Exports/GNP		GNP-corrected Exports/GNP	
	Coef-ficient	Signif-icance	Coef-ficient	Signif-icance	Coef-ficient	Signif-icance
Pre-World War I						
1877	−.109	.091	−1.00	.618	−.019	.608
1879	.042	.019	−3.86	.211	.049	.026
1884	−.094	.093	.38	.839	.006	.881
1885	.001	.571	−.74	.694	−.058	.196
1894	−.134	.020	4.56	.120	−.029	.336
1897	−.031	.258	1.67	.664	−.058	.101
1898	−.087	.044	−13.21	.014	−.009	.653
1904	−.053	.093	2.51	.247	−.014	.497
1906	.004	.728	−9.01	.009	−.015	.497
1907	.005	.651	−4.13	.037	−.014	.411
1909	−.073	.051	−.75	.681	−.044	.123
1912	−.061	.014	−2.48	.046	−.032	.052
1913	−.165	.000	−5.63	.001	−.081	.002
1914	−.007	.438	.74	.258	.006	.477
Interwar						
(1919)	.013	.348	—	—	.014	.308
(1920)	−.102	.007	—	—	−.063	.033
1931	−.027	.562	.38	.674	.004	.886
1932	.018	.664	−.44	.789	−.034	.501
(1935)	−.107	.274	−.01	.999	−.010	.867
1937	−.006	.848	.83	.482	.059	.221
1939	.088	.773	−2.18	.006	.071	.023
Post-World War II						
1948	.074	.529	—	—	.003	.794
1950	−.062	.023	—	—	−.023	.321
1956	−.134	.367	.132	.619	−.002	.875
1962	−.090	.010	−.002	.971	−.044	.144
1965	−.094	.002	−.374	.551	−.063	.017
1967	−.013	.415	−.028	.963	−.015	.351
1969	−.006	.715	.115	.895	−.009	.603
1971	−.048	.029	−.523	.628	−.036	.081
1973	−.011	.465	.157	.871	−.010	.501
1974	−.074	.625	.208	.815	−.008	.620

Note: The table shows the results of a bivaliate probit model estimated with trade data for the year prior to war, except 1919 and 1920, when data for 1920 are used. Data for Ethiopia is missing, so Italy is the only belligerent included for analysis of the 1935 Italo-Ethiopian War.

this period. It is also important to note that these war years also show a relative decline in exports in the preceding five-year period. Although big traders, exports were not growing prior to war.

Of the other governments deciding for war in this period, the insular Chinese traded least and went to war twice (1884 and 1894). Russia had next to the least trade and went to war three times (1877, 1904, and 1914). At the time of the Spanish-American War in 1898 the United States was the third-smallest exporter and Spain the fifth-smallest, although this relationship weakens when the large size of the U.S. economy is taken into account. The two Balkan Wars (1912 and 1913) are the most clear-cut instances of small traders going to war. In 1912, Bulgaria, Serbia, Greece, and Turkey were the first-, third-, fourth-, and sixth-*smallest* traders, respectively. Furthermore, the loss of trade during wartime is most evident, as the strongest relationship of the study exists for 1913 and the Second Balkan War, which uses data for the previous year affected by the First Balkan War.

This makes World War I an interesting case for further discussion. In August 1914, eight of the forty-two independent governments decided for war. Taken altogether, 1914 barely exhibits a negative relationship and a positive relationship emerges if economic size is taken into account, since the United Kingdom, Germany, France, Russia, and Austria-Hungary had very large economies. If we follow Bismarck's forecast and look to the war's Balkan origins, we find that the original two belligerents were comparatively small traders; Serbia was third-smallest and Austria-Hungary fourteenth-smallest. The rapid expansion to world war weakens the relationship because only Russia was also a small trader (eleventh-smallest). Two governments had large exporting economies: France was thirty-fifth from the bottom as the seventh-largest exporter. Belgium was the sixth-largest, although it was a victim of German aggression. For its part, Germany was a middle-range trader as eighteenth-smallest and Britain was twenty-fifth-smallest (eighteenth from the top). Japan, which joined later in August 1914, is the exactly median economy of the forty-one studied here. In short, like the preceding Balkan Wars, the First World War began between small-trading nations but quickly expanded to include large traders.

The relationships of the interwar period are by far the weakest and should not be unexpected, given the economic disruption in the world economy at the time. Only the 1920 war between the Soviet Union and Poland is accounted for with statistically significant results. Even though the analysis is peculiar (it is not performed with 1919 export percentages), it possesses considerable face validity given the isolation of the Soviet Union immediately after World War I and the newness of the Polish government and its national economy. The Soviet Union was by far the smallest trading economy at the time, and the Polish economy had the fourth-smallest export sector.

The two Sino-Japanese Wars of this period (1931 and 1937) are interesting in that one of the smallest traders, China, was the victim of aggression by one of the largest exporters; Japan was the seventh-largest exporter as a share of GNP in 1937. The independent actions by the imperialistic Japanese military overcame liberal civilian government and whatever constraint might have existed, especially since Japanese exports were growing at the time. Here, again, there is a Latin American war between trading nations. At the time of the Chaco War in 1932, Bolivia possessed an export economy, but Paraguay was more toward the bottom, especially considering the small size of its economy.

The stratification of nations beginning the Second World War in September 1939 is similar to the First World War. The original two belligerents were small exporters: Poland was fifth-smallest and Germany the eighth-smallest. As a result of trade frictions in the 1930s, France was no longer a large exporter, but was tenth-smallest. Of the fifty-three independent nations, the United Kingdom was in the middle (twenty-eighth-smallest). The Soviet Union, which invaded Poland in mid-September, was the smallest exporter as a share of GNP and also invaded Finland in November 1939. If analysis was confined to just these five nations, World War II would strongly fit the hypothesis, as only the United Kingdom is somewhat above the median. However, with the British declaration of war came decisions for war by four independent dominion governments that were all deeply involved in export trade: Australia (fifteenth-largest exporter), Canada (thirteenth), South Africa (fifth), and New Zealand (fourth). For these four governments, the obligation to Britain outweighed any constraint posed by foreign-trading interests, which might otherwise have felt that the promise of future trade profits rested with the fortunes of the British war against Germany. In other words, despite their rapid entry into war, they might better be considered joining belligerents and not original ones. Here, however, the standard of entry within one month will be preserved, although to some it might unreasonably affect the findings.

The most dramatic results are achieved for the period after the Second World War. Only one of ten war years (the 1948 Arab-Israeli War) is predicted in the opposite direction from what was expected in the theoretical arguments advanced earlier. All others (90%) are as hypothesized. Of the ten war years, the four Arab-Israeli Wars (1948, 1956, 1967, and 1973) show the weakest relationship, since the belligerent Arab nations and Israel are generally toward the average of exports as a share of GNP. Syria and Iraq were exceptions in 1948, when they exported a large share of total output. However, like the Latin American wars in the earlier periods, the exports of Middle Eastern Arab nations are heavily concentrated in primary products: Syrian cotton and Iraqi petroleum. Further, the 1969 Football War between El Salvador and Honduras is only weakly supportive of the hypothesis, which is consistent with earlier Latin American wars. The Turkish-Cyprus War of 1974 also shows a weak relationship, as the invasion victim, Cyprus, had a large export sector in its economy.

Very strongly negative relationships emerge for the wars in Asia. In the post–World War II era, belligerent Asian nations (North and South Korea, North and South Vietnam, China, India, and Pakistan) have been poor exporters. The United States, which fought in two Asian wars, did not possess a large export sector, although it is almost average when economic size is taken into account.

The most clear-cut war supporting the hypothesized relationship between trade and war is the Soviet-Hungarian War of 1956. Centrally planned economies of the 1950s had very little foreign trade, and no constraint from commercial interests existed.

Of the wars since 1975 not analyzed with a complete set of data, the Iran-Iraq War stands out as an exception in the post–World War II pattern. These two high-volume exporters of petroleum had large and rapidly expanding export sectors. As noted earlier, such high concentration in a single commodity qualifies any potential constraint, even though tangible export losses have damaged their economies. Of the other wars, Vietnam and Cambodia were extremely small exporters, while Ethiopia and Somalia were only somewhat larger. Uganda and Tanzania also had small export sectors, but when economic size is taken into account, Tanzania moves toward the top end of exporting nations. Finally, the United Kingdom was a high-exporting nation in 1982, when it went to war against small-exporting Argentina. The Falklands War then stands out as a major exception to the strong relationships since 1945.

Relationships between changes in trade prior to war years and decisions for war are much weaker on the whole and more varied (see the middle columns of table 5.2). What is striking, however, is that each and every instance that is estimated in a positive direction when analyzing the index of export percentages is predicted negatively by percentage change (1879, 1885, 1906, 1907, 1932, and 1939). Though the nations going to war in these years have larger export percentages, that percentage is declining (or increasing more slowly relative to other nations) in the five-year period prior to war. The relationship is statistically significant for three of these six war years. This finding is particularly meaningful for the beginning of World War II in 1939. Not all the governments deciding for war were less committed to trade as measured by exports as a percent of GNP, but this percentage was *declining* prior to the outbreak of war. Governments of nations deciding for war in 1939 had the fastest-shrinking export sectors! If these two variables, actual percentages and change before war years, are combined in a single model to predict decisions for war, little is gained, as the actual percentages generally predict far better than the variable recording change in the five-year period before war years.

The analysis of export percentages controlled by the size of national income (see the last columns of table 5.2) show weaker relationships, by and large, but as many are in the hypothesized relationship as for the analyses uncontrolled for economic size. A few relationships switch direction. The Sino-French War of 1884 now reflects a positive relationship, as expected given the size of the Chinese and French economies. The same occurs for the First World

War, which involved Europe's and the world's largest economies. The two Central American wars are predicted negatively here, as their exports are *less* than would be predicted on the basis of the small size of their economies. The relationship for the Sino-Japanese War is also accurately corrected through the consideration of economic size.

The relationships for the post–World War II years remain in the same direction as discovered for actual percentages of exports. They are, however, weaker in most instances. In short, the control for economic size was effective in that it reduced the strength of relationships and brought into line comparisons of nations with large differences in national income.

The support for the hypothesis that large traders are less inclined to wage war is buttressed when each of the periods is analyzed as a whole (the three anomalous interwar years excluded; see table 5.3). The strength of the relationships is enhanced by the use of additional degrees of freedom in aggregating the cases. Beyond that statistical reasoning, the very strong relationships in the hypothesized direction for both the actual export percentages and those controlling for size of national income in both the pre–World War I and post–World War II periods demonstrate the consistency of the negative relationship. For the more recent period, these findings indicate that there is only one one-thousandth of a chance that this negative relationship is attributable to chance.

CONCLUSIONS AND IMPLICATIONS

The results of the analysis reported in this chapter lead to rather obvious conclusions. First, the argument advanced in chapter 2 positing that governments of nations that are more involved in foreign trade are less likely to make decisions for war is supported. It is only in the period between the two world wars that no consistent relationship is discerned. This should by no means be unexpected given the awareness of the peculiar economic characteristics of the 1920s and 1930s.

The results also seem to indicate that the data generated to address the hypothesis are accurate indicators of exports as a percent-

TABLE 5.3   FOREIGN TRADE AND DECISIONS FOR WAR BY PERIOD

Period	Exports/GNP		Change in Export/GNP		GNP-corrected Exports/GNP	
	Coef-ficient	Signif-icance	Coef-ficient	Signif-icance	Coef-ficient	Signif-icance
1871–1914	−.011	.012	−.93	.009	−.009	.040
1919–1939	.004	.743	.20	.502	.021	.114
1948–1975	−.025	.001	−.00	.945	−.018	.002

age of GNP. The relationships that were uncovered are consistent with knowledge of world-trade patterns, and the success of the correction for economic size lends evidence to the viability of the raw data used in the analyses.

Some final comments in reference to change in the global system are possible. The hypothesized relationship between trade and war appears to have existed all along and was only interrupted by the First World War and the Depression of the 1930s. An alternative explanation would be that such a tendency on the part of governments exists only in times of economic prosperity. Change over time does not seem to have taken place in regard to the relationship between trade and war. In the length of time examined here, governments with a greater trade involvement are less likely to go to war in both the earliest and latest periods analyzed.

The findings here suggest that of the three sources of constraint by commercial interests, interpenetration is strongest. The growth of interpenetration suggests that growing foreign-trading sectors will create stronger domestic interest groups that wish to avoid war. Since negative relationships exist for the pre–World War I and post–World War II periods, the presence of a domestic foreign-trade sector would constrain governmental choice then and now. The reduced size of export sectors in the 1930s, when protectionism was strongest, indicates commercial interests would diminish in influence. The governments of the most vulnerable economies in the global system, those devoted to high exports of primary products,

138

were found to go to war often enough to make one doubt that inter-dependence, or independence, is the primary source of constraint on war. Finally, since negative relationships exist over a long time period, from 1871 to 1914 and from 1948 to 1975, the growing inter-connectedness of economies is not the main source of constraint, unless it is argued that a sufficient degree of interconnectedness already existed in the later nineteenth century, which may have in-deed been the case.

Further analysis of the relationship between foreign trade and war is called for. The findings here so clearly support the hypothesis that national governments that are more involved in trade are less inclined to make decisions for war that a clearer definition and understanding of the relationship is necessary.

6

INTERNATIONAL
INSTITUTIONS AND WAR

Having seen that international commerce has a
bearing on national decisions for war, we now turn to another potential constraint on the independent actions of national governments capable of waging interstate war: the conduct of international relations through international governmental organizations
(IGOs). IGOs are a particularly relevant manifestation of change in
the global system because they represent the alteration of traditional modes of interaction through the substitution of institutionalized multilateral relations for bilateral statecraft.

The replacement of the independent policies of national governments with the activities of collaborative organizations represents
an important potential constraint on decisions for war. In contrast
to the constraints of domestic political structure and foreign trade,
commitment to IGOs is directly manipulated by governments
themselves. Participation in international institutions is thus as
much an expression of disinclination to power politics and the use
of force as it is a constraint on government. As a national government divests itself of more of its independent prerogatives, it may
be that its capability and willingness to wage war decreases. This
can be seen to occur for two reasons, stemming from an unfolding
growth of functionalism (Mitrany, 1966). First, through international organizations, the possibility of mediating and resolving disputes before they reach the point of violence is greatly increased.
Indeed, several institutions—notably, the International Court of
Justice—exist solely for this purpose, and several more incorporate
this goal into their activities (the United Nations and Organization
for African Unity, for example). Second, the functional interdependencies of multilateral activity fostered by international organizations can be seen in many instances to have modified the structure

of national government so that to use force becomes more difficult in the face of conducting international relations through collaborative effort.

What follows is an attempt to discern the empirical validity of the hypothesis that greater participation in IGOs will decrease the likelihood of governments deciding to initiate war. Unfortunately, little research has been conducted on this question. The one notable study by Wallace and Singer (1970) examined IGO memberships and war involvement for an aggregate global system: for all independent governments in the global system without reference to those going to war and those remaining at peace.[1] Accordingly, the results of these analyses have shown no relationship. Harold Jacobson, however, observes that the average incidence of war for each government in the global system has declined since 1816, and this decline in systemic violence is associated with the secular rise in the cumulative number of IGO memberships (Jacobson, Reisinger, and Mathews, 1986).

The analyses that follow are based on comparisons of national memberships in IGOs. Since decisions for war represent the actions of individual national governments, ambiguous findings with system-level aggregations need not be indicative of relationships comparing the participation levels of individual governments. Comparisons themselves, moreover, need not be solely on the basis of national memberships in all kinds of organizations. IGOs devoted to security relations may have more bearing on decisions for war than those dealing with commercial or cultural exchanges. Indeed, there is good reason to suspect that participation in different types of IGOs will have a different effect on the propensities of governments to go to war.

FUNCTIONALISM, INTEGRATION, AND REGIONALISM

Several theoretical arguments account for the contribution of IGOs to international peace. The functionalist perspec-

1. See Singer and Wallace, "International Governmental Organization and the Preservation of Peace, 1816–1964: Some Bivariate Relationships," who found no relationship using rank order correlations for all nations in five-year periods between memberships and a variety of measures of war.

tive posits that the greater the amount of policy activity taking place in multilateral institutions, the greater the incentive to maintain cooperative relations between governments for the sake of achieving successful policy goals.[2] The more important the policy areas to the participating governments and the closer the agreement on policy objectives, the tighter the bonds between governments and the more likely a community of interest will stand in the way of war. Although such bonds may be modest at first, the spill-over to policy areas concerning security policy will eventually render the use of force impractical in the face of the collaborative management of key foreign-policy issues.

A second perspective is derived from the first. Neo-functionalism—or perhaps more accurately, political integration—argues that international organizations will eventually go beyond functional interdependencies and result in supranational institutions, or organizations with authority over national governments (Haas, 1958).[3] In short, international organization will replace the independent national government as the locus of policy-making in international relations. In the end, such institutions would be capable of preventing the use of force between governments participating in integration schemes.

However, little can be said of the war propensity of participants in integration arrangements with governments outside such institutions. On the one hand, if integration is structured as federalism, then decisions for war with governments outside the federation is feasible. On the other hand, neo-functionalism describes a qualitatively different political union, which emphasizes economic and social priorities at the expense of security concerns. Accordingly, the use of force by integrated governments is compromised. Put differently, federalism allows for power politics, albeit not among members of a federation, whereas neo-functional integration creates institutions incapable of pursuing policies associated with national interest and power politics.

Another perspective focuses on a particular type of organization,

2. The most notable example of this perspective is Mitrany, *A Working Peace System* (1966). See also Haas, *Beyond the Nation-State* (1964).

3. For a comparison of these two perspectives see Lindberg and Scheingold, *Europe's Would-Be Polity* (1970), chap. 1.

regional organizations with general purposes. Most of these IGOs, such as the Organization of American States or Council of Europe, have an explicit interest in resolving disputes between member governments before they cross the threshold of war. The success of these endeavors rests mainly on the community of interests formed by the group of governments in any region. The more cohesive the governments and the more they identify with common principles of interaction, the less the likelihood that conflicts between governments will result in war. The empirical evidence as to their record in peacefully settling disputes generally supports the notion that regional IGOs are conducive to peace and leads one to suspect that a direct relationship exists between participation in regional IGOs and the avoidance of war.[4]

All three of these postulated pacifistic effects of international organizations—functionalism, integration, and regionalism—rest on the notion of the development of a community of interests between the participating governments. Indeed, all three perspectives may correctly identify mutually reinforcing trends in international relations, because the growth of organizations of one type is likely to facilitate the development of other types.

All three trends, in addition, would lead one to suspect that organizations with memberships *limited* to governments that adhere to the community of interests embodied in a given organization are likely to reflect a commitment to multilateral collaboration and the existence of a constraint sufficient to dissuade member governments from initiating war. In other words, limited-membership IGOs constitute the type of institutions in which a community of interest is reflective of the trends of functionalism, integration, or regionalism. National participation in these IGOs, then, should constrain decisions for war.

The other type of international organization, of course, has a potentially universal membership. One could not expect the same

4. See the theoretical arguments developed by Nye, *Peace in Parts* (1971). For empirical findings relating to the success of international organizations in resolving interstate disputes see Haas, Butterworth, and Nye, *Conflict Management by International Organization* (1972); Butterworth, *Moderation from Management: International Organizations and Peace* (1978); and Zacher, *International Conflicts and Collective Security, 1946–1977* (1979).

kind of community of interests to develop across such a wider variety of independent governments. What may be provided, however, are global principles of collaboration. These types of IGOs were intended to embody universal norms for behavior, such as norms against genocide, colonialism, racism, and aggressive use of force. Universal-membership IGOs with a particular functional task provide a forum for the development of interdependence, although it is difficult to see how such organizations provide the same kind of bonds as limited-membership organizations where greater collaborative incentives exist between governments.

Having laid out the theoretical arguments behind participation in different types of international organizations, it is possible to proceed to the assessment of their validity through empirical analyses. The measurement of national participation in IGOs is not difficult. As institutions, IGOs are fairly easy to identify and membership is generally known. The identification of memberships has been made much easier by the work of the Union of International Associations, which publishes periodic editions of the *Yearbook of International Organizations* (Brussels: Union of International Associations, UIA). The task, then, is to count national memberships in IGOs according to various types as an indicator of national participation in international institutions. The following procedures were used here. First, a population of international IGOs (as opposed to non-governmental organizations) in existence in 1970 was taken from Appendix A of Harold K. Jacobson, *Networks of Interdependence* (1979). Only organizations with three or more independent national governments as members, regular meetings, and a permanent secretariat were counted. IGOs meeting these criteria and established since 1970 were identified with the use of the UIA's *Yearbook of International Organizations* (1978).

With this population of IGOs, national memberships can be coded for the date of entry and exit of each member government according to the information shown in various editions of the *Yearbook of International Associations*. Once the members of each organization and their dates of participation are coded, the participation in each type of organization can be counted for each year.

Despite the simplicity of this procedure, some distortion inevitably exists. Because the UIA gathers its data by periodic distribution of a questionnaire to organizations, there is some delay in the updating of memberships. Therefore, even an examination of each edition of the *Yearbook* would not precisely reflect memberships. Accordingly, several assumptions about membership were made here. First, when information to the contrary did not exist, members were coded as entering that IGO in the year in which an IGO was created. This is consistent with the tendency of the governments which participate in an IGO to immediately recognize the need for these institutions. Second, nations are coded as entering IGOs upon independence, unless otherwise indicated by the *Yearbook of International Associations.* Newly independent governments very quickly join IGOs that serve their interests and in many instances participated as observer or associate members before independence. Even if these two assumptions are accurate depictions of trends in IGO participation, there is bound to be some distortion in the data used here.

The above procedures identify over nine thousand memberships in IGOs existing since 1970. At least sixty-nine IGOs terminated before 1970. These IGOs, which were formed and disbanded prior to 1970, are identified in Michael D. Wallace and J. David Singer, "Intergovernmental Organization in the Global System, 1816–1964," (1970). Wallace and Singer identify memberships only by five-year periods, which reflects the difficulty of finding more precise information. Their data are corrected here according to the date of IGO establishment and extinction. All other memberships—those governments who joined after the creation of the IGO—are only coded according to the five-year period in which they became members. Therefore, their participation can be in error by no more than four years.

The memberships of several governments that are representative of the distribution of memberships in all types of IGOs are shown in table 6.1. Governments of industrialized nations belong to the most IGOs because of their greater economic and diplomatic activities. Centrally planned economies are restricted in their dealings in the world economy, given the non-convertibility of their currencies and the resulting difficulty of arranging trade with market economies. In addition, the foreign-policy orientations of these governments often lead to fewer commitments to organizations

TABLE 6.1   IGO MEMBERSHIPS FOR SELECTED GOVERNMENTS

Nation	1900	1935	1950	1970
Industrialized Nations				
France	23	52	80	131
Netherlands	20	43	72	120
United States	14	37	69	100
Japan	10	31	—	90
Switzerland	16	41	54	89
Centrally Planned Economies				
Serbia/Yugoslavia	11	43	50	79
Poland	—	34	39	62
Russia/U.S.S.R.	17	23	33	61
China	4	11	5	14
North Korea	—	—	5	12
Third World Governments				
Brazil	12	37	54	91
India	—	—	48	83
Egypt	—	—	42	79
Guatemala	4	23	40	73
Kenya	—	—	—	70
Nigeria	—	—	—	64
Haiti	6	20	37	61
Senegal	—	—	—	57
Philippines	—	—	29	57
Saudi Arabia	—	—	25	47

whose political activities differ from their ideological positions. China and North Korea have even fewer IGO memberships because of their less industrialized economies and their self-reliant strategies of development. However, China's status and participation in IGOs has changed dramatically since 1970, and other Third World governments are more involved in international organization, although less so than industrialized market-oriented states. Even so, their rate of participation varies widely (see also Jacobson et al., 1986). In short, participation in IGOs follows three general patterns that reflect the current division of the global system into three groups of governments with different policy objectives and orientations.

The growth of participation in IGOs is also quite steady. Only

TABLE 6.2 PARTICIPATION IN LIMITED AND UNIVERSAL-MEMBERSHIP
IGOS FOR SELECTED GOVERNMENTS

Nation	Membership Type	1900	1935	1950	1970
France	Limited	10	13	28	56
	Universal	13	39	52	75
United Kingdom	Limited	8	15	33	49
	Universal	12	33	47	72
United States	Limited	4	12	28	35
	Universal	10	25	41	65
Russia/Soviet Union	Limited	6	0	5	15
	Universal	11	23	28	46
China	Limited	0	3	0	3
	Universal	4	10	5	10
Brazil	Limited	2	10	16	31
	Universal	10	27	38	60
Thailand	Limited	0	1	3	15
	Universal	7	20	30	49
Egypt	Limited	—	—	5	37
	Universal	—	—	20	59
India	Limited	—	—	11	21
	Universal	—	—	37	62
Nigeria	Limited	—	—	—	15
	Universal	—	—	—	49

China narrowly *reduced* its IGO membership as a result of the
change to Communist leadership in 1949. Apart from a few cases,
most other governments have continually expanded their commitments to international organizations, with the exception of the interruptions caused by the two world wars (see also Jacobson, 1979,
chap. 3); a few governments with questionable status, notably Tai-
wan, have been excluded from many IGOs. In addition, the recent
moves by the U.S. and U.K. governments to leave selected IGOs
runs against the long-standing trend.

Table 6.2 lists the memberships of a sample of governments
in limited-membership and universal-membership IGOs. Because
there are more opportunities to join organizations open to all
governments, participation in universal-membership IGOs is far
greater than for limited-membership organizations.

With this data—counts of national IGO memberships by type of IGO—it is possible to analyze relationships to decisions for war. The hypothesis is that the greater the national participation in international institutions as measured by memberships in IGOs, the lesser the likelihood that a national government will resort to the sustained use of force to resolve international differences. Because the variables have the same properties as those analyzed in chapter 5, a dichotomous outcome predicted by a continuous variable, analyses here can proceed using the same probit models.

Table 6.3 displays the results of four sets of analyses for each year in which a war has occurred since 1870. Because so few international organizations existed before 1870, it makes little sense to analyze memberships because only a few governments belonged to more than one organization of any type.

With regard to membership in all types of IGOs, no strong relationships emerge, and very few relationships are statistically significant (probability of randomness less than .05). Only four of thirty-one (13%) relationships meet a criterion of a 95 percent significance level and, of these four, only two are in the hypothesized relationship. In short, there does not appear to be any relation between membership in IGOs, taken as an undifferentiated whole, and decisions for war. This is, of course, consistent with Wallace and Singer's findings using memberships aggregated to the system level.

The rate of acquisition of IGO memberships may also serve as a sort of early warning indicator. Since the growth of participation in IGOs has been quite steady since 1815, could it be that governments going to war have not been keeping up with trends toward international collaboration? In other words, governments that find it difficult to make additional commitments to international institutions might be the ones that find it easier to decide for war. This tendency is borne out in the findings reported in the second pair of columns in table 6.3, in which changes in memberships in the five years prior to each war year were compared. Twenty-one of twenty-seven (78%) of the comparisons are negative, indicating that governments going to war are decreasing—or more accurately, not increasing as fast as others—in their participation in IGOs. The results are by no means solid in that relationships are weak, but they suggest that governments going to war tend to lose interest in collaborative

TABLE 6.3　MEMBERSHIP IN IGOS AND DECISIONS FOR WAR

Year	Total Membership		Change in Total Membership		Limited-Membership IGOs		Universal-Membership IGOs	
	Coefficient	Significance	Coefficient	Significance	Coefficient	Significance	Coefficient	Significance
Pre–World War I								
1877	.271	.181	.32	.472	.334	.202	.305	.431
1879	−.382	.112	−.59	.214	−.889	.074	−.301	.428
1884	−.015	.903	.00	.999	.160	.476	−.094	.648
1885	−.883	.005	−1.85	.004	−.754	.085	−.757	.015
1894	−.099	.205	−.29	.220	−1.570	.003	−.067	.501
1897	.040	.557	.27	.504	.046	.766	.081	.471
1898	.085	.205	−.38	.479	.139	.286	.151	.208
1904	.013	.805	−.60	.077	−.062	.609	.068	.437
1906	−.236	.009	−.43	.107	−.157	.208	−.589	.002
1907	−.108	.061	−.08	.604	−.015	.876	−.376	.004
1909	−.012	.755	−.05	.654	.005	.956	.023	.672
1912	.020	.509	.14	.412	−.035	.665	.050	.672
1913	−.002	.946	−.00	.989	−.144	.124	.027	.519
1914	.077	.006	−.34	.038	.167	.013	.087	.019
Interwar								
1919	−.007	.821	—	—	−.125	.134	.042	.301
1920	−.011	.759	—	—	−.161	.151	.051	.287
1931	−.015	.538	−.25	.337	−.160	.077	−.003	.916
1932	−.010	.695	−.26	.403	.089	.237	−.032	.323
1935	−.002	.918	−.07	.772	−.020	.781	−.001	.984
1937	−.019	.454	−.07	.645	−.179	.058	−.005	.859
1939	.019	.242	−.26	.012	−.019	.619	.034	.092
Post–World War II								
1948	−.023	.171	—	—	−.150	.005	−.004	.850
1950	−.010	.517	—	—	.002	.955	−.002	.306
1956	.023	.038	.02	.660	−.031	.148	.045	.024
1962	−.013	.375	−.01	.883	−.031	.381	−.016	.438
1965	−.012	.246	−.10	.044	−.012	.620	−.024	.151
1967	−.001	.954	.00	.947	−.046	.101	.015	.344
1969	.002	.835	−.15	.164	.038	.122	−.017	.379
1971	.010	.364	−.31	.072	−.006	.842	.029	.117
1973	.005	.648	−.02	.775	−.024	.349	.024	.164
1974	.006	.594	−.01	.881	.003	.900	.014	.454

TABLE 6.4   MEMBERSHIP IN IGOS AND DECISIONS FOR WAR BY PERIOD

Period	Total Membership		Change in Total Membership		Limited-Membership IGOs		Universal Membership IGOs	
	Coef-ficient	Signif-icance	Coef-ficient	Signif-icance	Coef-ficient	Signif-icance	Coef-ficient	Signif-icance
1871–1914	.02	.068	−.09	.074	.02	.318	.03	.038
1919–1939	−.00	.824	−.10	.023	−.04	.087	.01	.318
1948–1975	−.00	.329	.00	.612	−.01	.071	−.00	.791

efforts. Two strongly negative relationships appear for 1914 and 1939, indicating the decreasing multilateralism of the governments entering both World Wars I and II.

As for the arguments of the functionalists, integrationists, and regionalists, the majority of comparisons for war years support the hypothesis of a negative relationship. Twenty-two of thirty-one (71%) relationships are negative, but they are also quite weak. Comparisons between participation in universal-membership IGOs and decisions for war are even less telling, as half the relationships are negative and half are positive.

The picture becomes clearer when the analyses are conducted for comparisons by historical period (see table 6.4). The results discussed above are confirmed. Relationships between changes prior to war years and decisions for war exist in the pre–World War I era and in the interwar period, but not since the Second World War. Clearly, this finding reveals the decline in the growth of participation in IGOs on the part of the governments initiating the two world wars. In fact, these periods before the two world wars mark the only significant interruptions in the growth of international institutions. Since the Second World War, there has been no such major curtailment in the interest of governments to participate in IGOs and, as a consequence, no consistent relationship exists. The ability to use channels in IGO membership as an early warning indicator will be explored later.

The findings for limited-membership IGOs are also interesting. Only the interwar and post–World War II periods have negative relationships, and they approach statistical significance. They are close enough to reflect the consistently negative patterns found in the analyses of each war year. In short, for these two periods, the arguments of the functionalists, integrationists, and regionalists seem to be supported. Governments with a greater participation in limited-membership IGOs—the kind that are likely to facilitate the development of a community of interest—less frequently decide for war.

Finally, analysis of universal-membership IGOs does show a significant positive relationship for the period leading up to the First World War. This should not be unexpected, as most organizations at this time were of this type. In addition, they were more heavily subscribed to by the larger and more diplomatically active governments of the era, which also—as captured by this coefficient—were more prone to wage war. For the other periods, no consistent relationship emerges.

To conclude, then, the analyses of changes in the five years prior to war years show a negative relationship that is consistent with the hypothesis, although it is largely a product of the two periods of slow or declining growth in IGOs before the two world wars. More importantly, participation in *limited*-membership IGOs is related in the hypothesized negative direction in the interwar and post–World War II periods. This, of course, when put in the context of the arguments advanced above, is consistent with the growth of functional interdependencies fostered by international institutions since 1919.

FUNCTIONAL ISSUES OF IGOs AND DECISIONS FOR WAR

In the development of IGOs the issue or policy content of new IGOs has tended to reflect the interests of governments in resolving certain problems of the day. The formation of IGOs thus constitutes a sort of international public-policy agenda. Could it be that participation in IGOs with different functional purposes will have different effects on decisions for war, depending on their relevance to issues of security?

The history of international organization captures the changing policy interests of the governments willing to coordinate actions in multilateral institutions. The first IGOs in the early nineteenth century addressed commercial issues, predominantly transportation and communication, and arrived hand in hand with the growth of free trade. It was only later that the first security and legal institutions were established to deal with the resolution of international disputes and the attempt to codify principles of international interaction. Social reforms in advanced industrial societies at the turn of the century led to creation of the first IGOs devoted to the betterment of social conditions. By the time of the First World War, all three types of IGOs existed. In the interwar period, few economic and social organizations were created because attention was focused on the general-purpose League of Nations and, later, to the resolution of political conflicts that led to the Second World War. Since World War II, all three types of IGOs have been formed, although the greatest growth has been in economic IGOs that address two major concerns: the maintenance of economic prosperity in industrialized economies and the attempt to redress economic inequalities between states.

IGOs with different purposes may have different relationships to decisions for war. Security and legal IGOs have an obvious link to war as a means either to resolve disputes peacefully or to provide deterrence to war through collective defense. In the aggregate, however, no relationship may appear. While some of these IGOs are directed toward the peaceful resolution of disputes between nations, others are designed as adversaries to another government or group of governments and may, therefore, contribute to international conflict. One would not necessarily expect different relationships, because the second type of collective defense IGO deters the use of force. Nonetheless, there exists a great diversity of aims in these types of IGOs.

It has already been shown that foreign trade acts as a constraint on decision for war (see chapter 5). It is likely, therefore, that participation in IGOs designed to facilitate international commerce would be negatively related to decisions for war. But the functional goals of commercial IGOs vary widely, and not all exist to facilitate trade. Many, in fact, exist to protect the economic advantages enjoyed by a few nations, which need not lead to reduced tensions and a constraint on decisions for war.

Finally, participation in IGOs dealing with social issues may be negatively related to decisions for war. Perhaps these IGOs represent the commitment of national governments to attaining social goals that might otherwise be sought solely through national means. In other words, governments with a greater involvement in IGOs dealing with social and cultural issues may be more interdependent and have weaker advocates of independent national action and power politics.

These three issue orientations of IGOs can be identified in the same manner as above. Six categories were used to code the policy area of each specific-purpose IGO: (1) security and legal, (2) trade and finance, (3) communications and transportation, (4) science and technology, (5) health and the environment, and (6) social and cultural issues. Categories two, three, and four have been coded as commercial IGOs, and the last two groups of organizations represent IGOs devoted to social concerns. Table 6.5 lists memberships in each type of IGO for the ten governments used for illustrative purposes above.

Following the procedures used above, table 6.6 displays the findings of analyses for each war year using national memberships in each issue-type of IGO. The findings for each category can be summarized briefly, as consistent relationships do not emerge. For each type of IGO, roughly half of the relationships are negative and the other half positive. Moreover, very few relationships are significant.

Analyzing these measures by period as shown in table 6.7 also indicates an absence of any relationship. Interestingly, there are some anomalously strong relationships for IGOs involved in social issues, but since the findings are in the opposite direction of the majority of relationships discerned in the analyses of war years, they are not indicative of any reliable relationship. In other words, little should be made of the negative relationship approaching significance for the post–World War II period, when only four of ten war years show relationships in that direction.

Analysis of IGOs by issue type reveals that membership does not affect decisions for war. Nevertheless, the analyses have uncovered

TABLE 6.5 MEMBERSHIPS IN IGOS BY ISSUE TYPE FOR SELECTED
GOVERNMENTS

Nation	Issue Type	1900	1935	1950	1970
France	Security	2	7	12	11
	Commercial	16	30	49	85
	Social	5	14	17	33
United Kingdom	Security	2	8	11	10
	Commercial	14	26	52	79
	Social	4	13	15	28
United States	Security	2	6	10	9
	Commercial	8	19	41	62
	Social	3	11	16	27
Russia/Soviet Union	Security	1	2	2	3
	Commercial	12	14	21	17
	Social	4	7	9	17
China	Security	1	2	0	0
	Commercial	3	4	1	8
	Social	0	4	2	5
Brazil	Security	2	5	6	6
	Commercial	8	18	29	50
	Social	1	12	17	32
Thailand	Security	1	4	4	5
	Commercial	5	8	17	36
	Social	1	8	11	20
Egypt	Security	—	—	7	8
	Commercial	—	—	23	47
	Social	—	—	10	21
India	Security	—	—	6	5
	Commercial	—	—	30	54
	Social	—	—	11	22
Nigeria	Security	—	—	—	4
	Commercial	—	—	—	39
	Social	—	—	—	19

some interesting relationships. In particular, changes in participation in IGOs are related to decisions for war in the two periods
marked by a decline in the rate of growth of international organization before the two world wars. More importantly, governments
that have participated in limited-membership IGOs since 1919 are
less likely to decide for war, a finding that supports the notions of
the functionalists, integrationists, and regionalists.

The results of the analyses for the entire period since 1945 show

TABLE 6.6   MEMBERSHIP IN IGOS BY FUNCTION AND DECISIONS FOR
WAR

MEMBERSHIP BY IGO FUNCTION

	Security		Commercial		Social	
Year	Coef-ficient	Signif-icance	Coef-ficient	Signif-icance	Coef-ficient	Signif-icant
Pre–World War I						
1871	—	—	.421	.167	.411	.334
1879	—	—	−.411	.233	−1.152	.082
1894	—	—	−.014	.934	.065	.858
1885	—	—	−1.209	.004	−1.072	.089
1894	.103	.878	−.115	.283	−.399	.166
1897	.125	.852	.045	.646	.290	.223
1898	1.623	.063	.091	.316	.276	.226
1904	.262	.636	.041	.589	−.040	.814
1906	−.575	.269	−.695	.001	−.318	.117
1907	−.575	.269	−.194	.042	−.287	.073
1909	−.370	.443	.043	.484	.005	.961
1912	.400	.382	.036	.464	.049	.501
1913	−.009	.984	−.004	.932	.021	.781
1914	.245	.493	.155	.001	.155	.024
Interwar						
1919	−.372	.223	.031	.513	.013	.870
1920	−.177	.346	.055	.323	−.040	.732
1931	−.181	.239	−.020	.609	−.028	.725
1932	−.040	.801	−.050	.265	.042	.639
1935	−.045	.775	.004	.911	−.036	.629
1937	−.185	.230	−0.034	.449	−.029	.728
1939	.111	.251	.054	.049	−.019	.705
Post–World War II						
1948	−.092	.363	−.037	.166	−.099	.112
1950	−.062	.505	−.006	.811	−.073	.233
1956	.127	.151	−.041	.012	.025	.568
1962	−.208	.137	−.011	.616	−.067	.198
1965	−.122	.211	−.012	.478	−.054	.122
1967	−.022	.809	−.002	.878	.005	.883
1969	.089	.443	−.013	.538	.006	.171
1971	.034	.783	.017	.306	.030	.480
1973	.097	.374	.008	.582	.003	.939
1974	.072	.542	.007	.701	.024	.564

TABLE 6.7   MEMBERSHIP IN IGOS BY FUNCTION AND DECISIONS FOR
WAR BY PERIOD

MEMBERSHIP BY FUNCTION

	Security		Commercial		Social	
Period	Coef-ficient	Signif-icance	Coef-ficient	Signif-icance	Coef-ficient	Signif-icance
1871–1914	.147	.147	.026	.093	.053	.029
1919–1939	−.022	.623	.013	.326	−.012	.635
1948–1975	−.011	.740	−.003	.545	−.020	.070

that for each indicator of IGO participation—for all IGOs, for membership types, and for issues types—the relationships are negative,
although only two approach significance. If participation in international organization continues unabated, as it has since the Second World War, could one expect a more significant threshold to be
reached as even more international relations are conducted in international institutions? In other words, the analyses conducted here
may tap only the beginnings of the influence of international organization on international politics. With the continued growth of the
activities of IGOs, the truly effective constraints on war-making potential of national governments may be yet to come.

7

THE IMPACT
OF CHANGE ON
DECISIONS FOR WAR

Several relationships exist between trends of change in the global system and decisions for war, and although not all the indicators examined previously were found to be significant, a number provide empirical evidence of the importance of changing factors to governments capable of going to war. These changing aspects of international relations were introduced as being complementary and potentially cumulative in their effect on the politics of war and peace. Accordingly, it is important to consider the explanatory power of a combination of these more meaningful trends as a means better to understand decisions for war.

A COMBINED-EFFECTS MODEL

Only a few indicators—those that predict a consistent relationship between individual trends and decisions for war—are appropriate for inclusion in a multivariate model. As for the importance of domestic political structure to decisions for war, no strong relationships were found. In fact, what relationships existed contradicted the hypothesized notion that greater amounts of domestic political activity in the domestic environment of national governments were conducive to peace. Although part of this tendency can be accounted for by considering the issue over which governments actually exerted sustained force, could it be that domestic political structure has a different or even stronger effect on decisions for war when other factors are considered?

To answer this question, an indicator of the degree of openness in domestic political structure must be included in a multivariate model. Even though two aspects of domestic structure were analyzed in chapter 4 (limits on executive authority and the extent of political competition), a single indicator can be used. Because each of these variables was measured with four-level ordinal scales, the indicator included here must reflect the presence of either or both. With that in mind, a binary variable differentiating between governments with total limits on the authority of the executive *or* with institutionalized political competition is used here. This single binary variable accurately summarizes levels of openness. In the period since 1870, 30 percent of the nation-years can be coded as one, meaning that they were characterized by either complete limits on executive authority or institutionalized political competition. Of course, most nations (78 percent) in this group possess both attributes.

Whereas domestic political structure was not seen to be significantly related to decisions for war in the bivariate analyses conducted in chapter 4, the findings concerning the role of foreign trade indicated a consistently negative relationship between exports as a percentage of national economic output and decisions for war. Governments of national economies that are more involved in foreign trade are less inclined to initiate war. This conclusion is valid for two indicators: exports as a percent of GNP and the percentage difference from what would be expected, given the inverse relation of exports to economic size. This second indicator controlling for the size of the domestic market is not as strongly related to decisions for war as the actual share of exports in GNP, but accurately removes the distorting effects of large economies needing to trade less to maintain prosperity. Accordingly, only this second indicator of the involvement of national economies in international commerce will be included in a multivariate model. Not only does it control for size, which makes it more theoretically meaningful in several respects, but it is also a more conservative measure, as the bivariate investigations showed it to be less strongly related to decisions for war. The model examined here should not be loaded with variables used merely to account for greater variance in the outcome variable. With the use of this variable, there is a lesser chance that any conclusions as to the negative relationship of trade to war can be made erroneously. As in chapter 5, trade in the year prior to the outbreak of war must be used for analysis.

The analysis conducted in chapter 6 indicated that two aspects of the growth of international organizations are related to war onset. First, because of the decline in the rate of growth of IGOs prior to the two world wars, the change in memberships in the five-year period prior to each war year is a meaningful variable. When included in a multivariate model, it should be negatively related to decisions for war in the pre–World War I and interwar eras, but not in the post–World War II period, when the pace of growth in IGOs has been quite steady for almost every nation. It is only in the two earlier periods that states going to war experience declines or slower growth in their participation in international institutions.

Second, participation in limited-membership IGOs was discovered to be somewhat negatively related to decisions for war in the interwar and post–World War II periods, a finding that supports the arguments of the functionalists, integrationists, and regionalists. Accordingly, a variable measuring the number of national memberships in such organizations can be added to the model examined here as a potentially potent explanatory variable.

Whereas any number of variables can be analyzed in a multivariate model, only those that have been discovered to provide some useful explanatory information should be included. Not only will findings be confused by incorrect model specification, but the superfluous variables detract from the significance of the truly meaningful indicators of change in the global system. These four variables constitute the set of factors of change for which their cumulative effect can be usefully examined in a single explanatory model. The functional form of the model to be examined here is: Decisions for War = f (Open Domestic Political Structure, Exports as a Percent of GNP, Change in Total IGO Memberships, Participation in Limited-Membership IGOs).

This model can be estimated using the probit techniques investigating bivariate relationships, as the outcome variable remains dichotomous and the predictors are continuous variables. Just as a chain is as strong as its weakest link, the estimation of a multivariate model is constrained by its most limiting variable: data for all five variables must be present to estimate each war year. The absence of data on changes in total IGO membership and the incomplete export figures in 1919 and 1920 means that three war years (1919, 1920, and 1948) must be excluded from multivariate analysis.

Otherwise, the analysis of this multivariate model can be conducted in the manner used for the bivariate investigations. The major difference between the two types of probit models lies in the significance of the estimated parameters (coefficients) and the explanatory power of the model itself. Because five parameters must be estimated—one for each variable plus a constant term—greater degrees of freedom are necessary. In other words, because each variable must compete with the rival explanatory variables in the model, to be statistically significant it must account for a substantially different amount of the variance in the outcome variable than the other three predictor variables in the model.

Since these trends were selected because of their complementary nature, statistically significant relationships should be fairly rare, as a certain common variance is explained by several indicators; for example, exports and membership in limited-membership IGOs are interrelated. This issue is analogous to the problem of multicollinearity in econometric modeling using least-squares estimating techniques. While the features of probit analysis are yet to be fully explored by statisticians, for whom it remains a fairly new mode of analysis, the intercorrelation of predictor variables need not produce distortions in estimated parameters. This stems from the probit's use of an iterative search procedure to find optimal parameter values as opposed to the matrix manipulations of least squares algorithms, for which assumptions of uncorrelated predictor variables are restrictive.

Estimated parameters should also be less significant than those found in bivariate analyses because the ratio of coefficients to cases is increased. In other words, the same number of cases (data for each national government) must be used to estimate three additional parameters. Accordingly, significance levels as determined by the standard error of estimate for each coefficient will be higher, and fewer parameters should reach the criterion of 95 percent certainty.

In terms of the performance of the model as a whole in discriminating between governments going to war and those remaining at peace, significance levels need not be similar to those found for bivariate relationships. Since more variables are used to differentiate the actions of governments, explanatory power should be enhanced. But the model itself will be more significant than the bivariate relationships only if the added explanatory power is greater than what would be expected through the addition of variables. The degrees of freedom necessary to estimate more parameters in a larger model compensates for the greater information of a multivariate model in the calculation of significance levels and, hence, a determination of the explanatory power of the model.

With these considerations in mind, it is possible to examine the results of estimation using the probit techniques on the model developed above. Table 7.1 displays the coefficients derived from estimation of the model for each war year.

As anticipated, there are very few statistically significant coefficients. The model as a whole performs reasonably well as seven of twenty-eight (25%) estimations pass the threshold of 95-percent significance level and an additional four meet a 90-percent criterion (a total of 40%). Only five estimations (18%) reflect a poor performance of the model, producing estimates that are less than 50 percent certain.

The estimated coefficients summarize quite accurately the findings of the bivariate analyses. For the binary variable measuring open domestic political structures, the values are generally positive, meaning that more "democratic" governments (coded one) tend to wage war more often than other governments. This relationship is more consistent in later periods, as not a single negative coefficient is estimated in the period after the Second World War; it also concurs with the conclusions of chapter 4, in which bivariate relationships were explored.

Similarly, the coefficients for exports as a percentage of GNP (controlling for size) are consistently negative in the pre–World War I and post–World War II periods, as were the findings of bivariate investigations. This finding reinforces the conclusion that nations that are more involved in international commerce are less likely to decide for war, even when other changing factors are taken into account.

161

TABLE 7.1 ADDITIVE EFFECTS OF CONSTRAINTS ON DECISIONS FOR WAR

Year	Political Partici- pation	Exports as Percent of GNP	Change in Total IGO Membership	Participation in Limited- Membership IGOs	Signif- icance
Pre–World War I					
1877	−1.56	−.08	.28	.65	.258
1879	−1.44	−.07	.72	−1.15	.074
1884	.58	−.00	−.37	.21	.895
1885	.00	−.12	−2.02	−.22	.037
1894	1.34	−.01	.17	−1.65*	.035
1897	.83	−.10	.37	.08	.279
1898	2.15	−.08	−3.79*	.90	.011
1904	1.75	.01	−1.94	.51	.075
1906	−1.86	−.01	−.49	.01	.312
1907	−1.69	−.01	−.11	.09	.581
1909	.98	−.06	−.25	.24	.327
1912	.27	−.04	.14	.09	.434
1913	.42	−.09	.11	−.11	.023
1914	1.33*	−.00	−.53*	.13	.006
Interwar					
1931	.04	.00	.11	−.29	.233
1932	−1.17	−.01	−.28	.09	.426
1935	−1.39	.01	−.28	.09	.591
1937	−.65	.09	.00	−.32	.106
1939	.30	.05	−.21	−.24	.034
Post–World War II					
1950	.95	−.04	−.04	.13	.188
1956	.24	−.04	−.00	.03	.649
1962	.98	−.05	.05	−.06	.328
1965	.34	−.08	−.12	.04	.059
1967	.22	−.01	.12	−.11*	.158
1969	.21	−.01	−.24	.05*	.177
1971	1.74	−.06	−.15	−.01	.027
1973	.18	−.01	−.01	−.03	.763
1974	1.44*	−.02	−.02	−.02	.259

*Statistically significant to the 95-percent level.

TABLE 7.2 ADDITIVE EFFECTS OF CONSTRAINTS ON DECISIONS FOR
WAR BY PERIOD

Period	Political Participation	Exports as Percent of GNP	Change in Total IGO Membership	Participation in Limited-Membership IGOs	Significance
1871–1914	.337* (.187)	−.013* (.006)	−.186* (.063)	.079* (.031)	.002
1919–1939	.062 (.272)	.020 (.016)	−.073 (.060)	−.043 (−.031)	.155
1948–1975	.550* (.202)	−.025* (.009)	−.000 (.013)	−.005 (.009)	.003

*Statistically significant to the 95-percent level.
Standard error of estimate is shown in parentheses.

The coefficients for change in total IGO memberships differ somewhat from those found in bivariate analyses. They are more consistently negative, especially in the post–World War II era, where no
such relationship was found. They are quite weak, however, and it
is perhaps best to conclude that no relationship exists.

For the variable measuring the participation of governments in
limited-membership IGOs, the relationships portrayed by the coefficients are not nearly as negative as those in bivariate analyses.
Negative relationships still number more than positive ones in the
later two periods, and they are stronger with the passage of time.
This, of course, was also the finding of bivariate analysis in chapter 6.

The similarity of the multivariate findings to those from bivariate
analyses is even more evident when the model is estimated for the
three historical periods (see table 7.2). The aggregation of cases by
period should increase the statistical significance of coefficients. All
the coefficients for the first period are statistically significant,
whereas none are for the interwar period, and only the first two are
in the model for the most recent period.

The ability of the four variables to discriminate between governments deciding for war and remaining at peace is very good for the
pre–World War I period and post–World War II era, as was generally
true of the analyses by period for bivariate relationships.

As in bivariate analyses, greater openness of domestic political structure is positively related to decisions for war, especially in the post–World War II period, whereas foreign trade is strongly and negatively related to war in the first and last of the three periods. Change in total IGO membership is negatively related to war initiation, but only very weakly so since World War II. Finally, in the two periods since the First World War, greater participation in limited-membership IGOs is negatively related to decisions for war. As in the bivariate findings, these relationships only approach statistical significance. Before the First World War, membership in such IGOs is positively related to the onset of war, which is a reflection of the greater involvement of the more diplomatically active and more war-prone governments in the early development of limited-membership organizations.

INTERACTION EFFECTS

The similarity of the results of analysis using a multivariate model and those examining bivariate associations is to be expected if the predictor variables measure sufficiently distinct trends and they are considered additively, that is, as individual explanatory variables and not as the joint effect of levels in two or more trends. By including interaction effects in the model presented above, the cumulative impact of combinations of more than one variable can be investigated.

In terms of model specification, this can be simply accomplished by the addition of variables representing the product of two or more variables (Kmenta, 1971, chap. 11). The coefficient for this multiplicative term can be evaluated in the same manner as the coefficients for variables measuring the individual trends. The effect their inclusion has on the estimated parameters for other variables in the model will be of particular interest. If their significance is substantially less than their component parts, then it is possible to conclude that no interaction effect exists. If, on the other hand, these multiplicative terms do as well or better than the variables that comprise them, then interaction effects have been discovered, and their meaning can be interpreted in the context of the theoretical discussions developed earlier.

But which interactions should be included? With the four variables used above, eleven combinations of two or more variables are possible. Clearly, including more than a very few will make the interpretation of coefficients difficult, because the several multiplicative terms using the same components will be very similar and the effects of any one term will be difficult to ascertain. Also, the addition of many terms will drastically increase the expense of estimating parameters with the interactive search that is called for by the use of probit models. More importantly, however, theoretical arguments should support the inclusion of particular interaction effects if interpretation of findings is to be meaningful. Thus, only two multiplicative variables will be added to the multivariate model.

Since the arguments for suspecting a negative relationship between involvement in foreign trade and decisions for war concerned the development of domestic interest groups opposed to war and able to influence national policies, there should be an interaction between trade activity and the openness of the domestic political system. Perhaps political openness constrains decisions for war only when a strong interest group opposed to war is present to take advantage of openness. Therefore, the combination of these two factors should yield additional explanatory power (this is accomplished by simply multiplying the two variables). Since the measure of domestic political structure is binary, coded zero and one, the product of the two variables will be zero if there is a closed political structure and the value for exports as a percentage of GNP if there is a high degree of political participation.

A second interaction term is composed of exports as a percentage of GNP and participation in limited-membership IGOs. Both of these variables measure different aspects of the commitment of any government to cooperative relations between governments—one through the necessarily reciprocal nature of foreign trade and the other through the collaborative nature of policy coordination in international institutions. The combination of these two important commitments to cooperative foreign policies can be expected to jointly affect the willingness of the government to go to war, and the product of these two variables is added to the multivariate model.

One other interaction effect is possible. An "open communication" hypothesis argues that open political structures and public diplomacy in the forums of international organizations interact to make the use of force by sovereign states difficult (see Jacobson et al., 1986). But preliminary investigations of this interaction effect show that it possesses no explanatory power and that its inclusion in a multivariate model is unwarranted.

The addition of these two interaction terms allows analysis to proceed along the lines used in estimating a strictly additive model. Table 7.3 shows the results of estimation for each war year.

The incorporation of interaction terms has indeed modified the relationships found in the additive model; many of the estimated parameters have changed in the direction of the relationship. In addition, the performance of the model is slightly weaker, indicating that the inclusion of two interaction terms does not compensate for the need to estimate two additional parameters. On the whole, they are quite significant, warranting the interpretation of the coefficients as being meaningful contributions to the explanatory power of the model.

Surprisingly, the direction of the relationships for each variable is more mixed than before—that is, the coefficients for domestic structure are less consistently positive and those for exports as a percentage of GNP less consistently negative. The coefficients for the multiplicative variables are more consistently negative than the others, indicating that the arguments for their inclusion are valid.

There is, however, greater variance in the strengths of relationship as indicated by the significance of the coefficients—there are more very strongly significant coefficients, but also more very weak relationships. Accordingly, the interpretation of findings based on the analysis of war years is limited. More precise conclusions as to the presence of interactions among variables can be drawn from the analysis of the model by period, where tendencies in the direction and strength of relationships can be confirmed with more statistical confidence.

Table 7.4 contains the estimates of the parameters for the interactive model by each period. Indeed, the changing direction of relationships in the analyses for war years were illusory. Specifically, the relationship of domestic political participation to decisions for war remains positive. The negative relationships in the analysis of

TABLE 7.3 INTERACTIVE EFFECTS OF CONSTRAINTS ON DECISIONS FOR WAR

Year	Political Partici-pation	Exports as % GNP	Change in Total Member-ship	Limited Member-ship	Participa-tion × Exports	Limita-tions × Exports	Signif-icance
Pre–World War I							
1877	−1.00	.01	.22	.23	.01	−.05	.448
1879	−1.92	.07	.75	−.92	−.04	.04	.199
1884	.41	−.01	−.34	.23	−.01	.01	.979
1885	4.78	−.19	−2.48	−.33	.36	−.05	.098
1894	.68	−.04	.05	−1.36	−.10	.04	.099
1897	−.33	−.02	.27	−.06	−.17	−.01	.283
1898	2.18	.02	−3.34	.84	−.05	−.02	.034
1904	1.80	.02	−1.92*	.52	−.01	−.00	.202
1906	−1.91	−.01	−.51	.02	.02	.00	.572
1907	−1.62	.02	−.09	.13	.04	−.01	.691
1909	1.21	−.05	−.25	.23	.03	−.01	.558
1912	−1.80	−.20*	.20	.11	−.18*	.03*	.012
1913	−1.39	−.14*	.10	.01	−.14	−.01	.022
1914	1.38*	−.02	−.62	.09	−.05	.01	.010
Interwar							
1931	−.09	.04	.11	−.30	−.03	−.01	.464
1932	−1.68	.24	−.32	.02	−.09	−.03	.576
1935	−1.97	.26	−.53	−.02	−.16	−.03	.728
1937	−2.77	.51	−.21	−.60*	−.28	−.05	.131
1939	.43	.01	−.19	−.02	.02	.01	.101
Post–World War II							
1950	.77	.06*	.01	.09	.02	−.01	.280
1956	−.35	−.05	.01	.06	−.08	.01	.528
1962	.03	−.06	.04	−.02	−.13	.01	.486
1965	.79	−.11*	−.10	.05	.05	.00	.130
1967	.29	.02	.13	−.13*	.03	−.00	.272
1969	.29	.01	−.24	.05*	.00	−.00	.353
1971	.85	−.04	−.15	−.00	−.14*	.00	.035
1973	.15	.03	.01	−.04	.03	−.00	.705
1974	1.41*	.03	.02	−.01	−.01	−.00	.401

*Statistically significant to the 95-percent level.

TABLE 7.4   INTERACTIVE EFFECTS OF CONSTRAINTS ON DECISIONS
FOR WAR BY PERIOD

Period	Political Partici- pation	Exports as % GNP	Change in Total Member- ship	Limited Member- ship	Partici- pation × Exports	Limita- tion × Exports	Signif- icance
1871– 1914	.235 (.195)	−.013* (.008)	−.196* (.064)	.087* (.033)	−.027* (.014)	.002 (.002)	.002
1919– 1939	.099 (.326)	.017 (.050)	.074 (.061)	.043 (.038)	.012 (.043)	−.001 (.005)	.324
1948– 1977	.473* (.209)	−.015 (.016)	−.001 (.013)	−.007 (.010)	−.015 (.019)	−.000 (.001)	.009

*Statistically significant to the 95-percent level.
Standard error of estimate is shown in parentheses.

individual war years for this variable were quite weak, whereas the positive ones were much stronger, producing a positive relationship in the aggregate. The same is true, although in reverse, for exports as a percentage of GNP.

The strength of the relationship for these two variables is, however, significantly weaker than in the additive model previously estimated. This is due to the presence of the interaction term consisting of the combined effect of political participation and export activity. The coefficient for the product of these two variables is significant for the period before the First World War but not in later periods. Just as important is the reduced significance of the coefficients for the two component variables. The interaction term is more significant than either component in the period leading up to World War I and as significant as trade activity in the period since World War II. In short, for these two periods, the interaction of domestic structure and exports as a percentage of GNP adds to the explanatory power of the model. More importantly, the estimated parameter depicts a negative relationship, whereas one component is positively related to decisions for war. Therefore, it is possible to conclude that an open domestic political structure is a constraint on decisions for war, but only for governments in which a sizable portion of the economy is oriented toward foreign trade. This was the argument that called for the investigation of an interaction effect.

The same cannot be said for the interaction of trade activity with participation in limited-membership IGOs. The coefficients for the product of these two variables do not approach significance in any period. In addition, the estimated parameters for the variable measuring IGO memberships are not much changed from those found in the additive model. In short, no interaction effect exists based on these two variables.

In conclusion, whereas the findings from the estimation of the additive effects of trends in the global system merely confirmed the results of bivariate analyses, the investigation of interaction effects yields additional insights. Specifically, the cumulative effect of greater openness in political structures and export activity is negatively related to war. Governments that conduct larger amounts of export trade and possess a more open domestic political structure are less likely to go to war. It is only in combination with a large trading sector of the economy that political structure leads to an effective constraint on the war-making propensities of independent national governments.

8

WAR AND THE
CHANGING GLOBAL SYSTEM

The most likely sources of constraint on governmental choice derive from the areas of greatest change in the global system, and the constraints studied here—domestic political structure, foreign trade, and international organization—have long been argued as leading governments away from war. In this book, the most durable finding describes a significantly decreased tendency to decide for war by governments of economies with larger foreign-trading sectors. Further, since 1945, a greater participation in limited-membership international organizations is slightly associated with an avoidance of war. However, contrary to theoretical expectations, more "open" political systems exhibit an increased tendency to wage war. This finding is somewhat mediated by the interaction of trading involvement with an open political system, since the presence of both a trading commitment and more open system poses an additional degree of constraint.

The fuller meaning and implication of these findings can be further explored through the direct comparison of decisions for war. Table 8.1 lists forty-three decisions for war in the period from 1871 to 1914, categorized according to levels of the three variables characteristic of constraint on decisions for war. Domestic structures are shown to be either "open" or "closed," based on the indicator constructed for the analyses in chapter 7. Governments are grouped into the bottom, middle, or top third of a rank order of participation in limited-membership IGOs, which was shown in chapter 6 to be mildly indicative of a constraint on war. Likewise, governments are grouped into three levels of foreign-trading involvement, taken as exports as a share of GNP, controlling for the size of the economy. Controlling for economic size is a more conservative indicator of foreign trade, but suitably corrects for the pattern of less trade by

TABLE 8.1 DECISIONS FOR WAR, 1871–1914, CATEGORIZED ACCORDING TO LEVELS OF TRADE, IGO PARTICIPATION, AND OPEN OR CLOSED POLITICAL SYSTEM

Low IGO Membership		Medium IGO Membership		High IGO Membership	
Closed	Open	Closed	Open	Closed	Open
Low Export					
China '84	Japan '94	Turkey '77		Turkey '97	Spain '98
Guatem. '85	Greece '97	El Salvador '06		Nicaragua '07	Spain '09
El Salvador '85	Serbia '12	Honduras '06			
China '94	Greece '12	El Salvador '07			
Morocco '09	Serbia '13	Honduras '07			
Bulgaria '12	Greece '13	Turkey '11			
Bulgaria '13	Serbia '14	Turkey '12			
		Turkey '13			
		Romania '13			
Medium Export					
Chile '79	Japan '04		U.S. '98	Russia '07	
Guatemala '06	Japan '14			Russia '04	
				Austria '14	
				Russia '14	
High Export					
Bolivia '79				Italy '11	France '84
				Germany '14	France '14
					U.K. '14
					Belgium '14

larger economies, as was shown in chapters 5 and 7. Accordingly, some of the comparisons discussed here differ from observations made in chapter 5, where decisions for war were also studied without correction for economic size. These categorizations are for the years in which decisions for war were made and not for the period as a whole.

The distribution of decisions for war across these categories matches the findings in the previous chapters. First, sixteen of forty-three (37%) decisions are by governments with "open" domestic structures. Since the average proportion of "open" domestic structures in this period is 31 percent, this shows a slightly greater tendency of these governments to decide for war. Even with the more conservative control for economic size, there are far more decisions for war by governments with economies marked by small export sectors: twenty-seven (63%) war decisions are by governments in the bottom third of trading nations, nine (21%) by governments in the middle third, and seven (16%) in the top third. This displays the strong negative relationship between foreign-trade involvement and decisions for war found in chapter 5. Finally, for this period, chapter 6 revealed that membership in limited-membership IGOs was not related to decisions for war, and that finding is echoed here with governmental decisions not ordered by levels of membership: nineteen (44%) in the bottom third, ten (23%) in the middle third, and fourteen (36%) in the top third. As in earlier analyses, only the patterns of lesser trading nations deciding for war more often is apparent.

However, the conventional distinction of great power marks a group of governments categorized in the top third of both IGO membership and exports. The late-nineteenth-century European powers—Britain, France, Germany, Italy, Russia, and Austria-Hungary—are all located together toward the lower right-hand corner of the table. Since economic size is taken into consideration (in fact, Russia is the second-smallest trader if economic size is not taken into account), the larger economies need not export as large a portion of their GNP to be placed in this category. More to the point, however, the size of the export sector is synonomous with the level of industrialization, which is an attribute closely associated with power in world politics. In other words, the higher levels of industrialization in this era placed these nations at the center of world power and world trade. Russia and Austria-Hungary were both less industrialized than the other four European powers, and they also traded less. The link to industrialization is also indicated by Belgium's appearance in this group as a highly industrialized trading nation, hardly a great power but the victim of Germany's 1914 invasion. These European governments were also very active in international organizations, which fits the diplomatic role associated with the great powers.

The rising world powers of Japan and the United States are not grouped with the European powers. The United States, at the time of its only decision for war in this period (1898), was in the middle of the distribution—an average trader considering its position as the world's largest economy and a member of an average number of limited-membership, mostly Pan-American international organizations. Japan, on the other hand, decided for war three times. It was not a member of any limited-membership international organizations, because Asia possessed only a few otherwise antagonistic independent governments. In this period of rapid Japanese economic growth and industrialization, the first decision for war (1894) finds Japan in the bottom third of trading economies, but the two later decisions for war were taken when Japan had moved into the middle third. As we shall see, continued industrialization and trade places Japan toward the top of all trading nations at the time of its next decision for war in 1931. The speed and timing of industrialization and expansion of the export sector is related to Japanese decisions for war, which are more frequent in comparison to the other great powers. Russia's three decisions for war might also be associated with its later and rapid rate of industrialization toward the end of the nineteenth century.

Of the forty-three decisions for war in the 1871–1914 period, eighteen (42%) were made by Balkan nations (including Russia); a total of nine decisions for war were taken by the participants in the two Balkan Wars alone (1912 and 1913). In fact, these two wars most closely resemble the theoretical expectations: the participating governments were near the bottom of foreign-trading economies and had very few memberships in international organizations. However, since Greece and Serbia were comparatively democratic, domestic political structure is not a common element, unless one posits common domestic political characteristics of Balkan nations not studied here.

The Balkan character of World War I can be further explored, since the eight decisions by governments to wage war stand out as contrary to theoretical expectations. Serbia, a Balkan belligerent of the previous two years, links the three wars together. But the other belligerents stand out as large traders committed to international organization. By controlling for economic size, Russia and Austria-Hungary are promoted from the bottom ranks of trading nations, but the decisions by Germany, France, and Great Britain remain as exceptions to the overall finding of large trade as a constraint on

173

war (Belgium's victimization by Germany is easy to explain). As an exception nonetheless, the rapid unfolding of a Balkan crisis until war included the European great powers and Japan is a graphic demonstration of the relevance of power politics with its emphasis on contests of military capability and alliance. Therefore, it is a noteworthy finding that constraints on war are not universal. Circumstances of political rivalry, threat, and insecurity are not constrained by actors, interests, or avenues that in other situations might prevent decisions for war. The analysis of World War I shows that the security interests associated with power politics are difficult to overcome by potential constraints on choice.

Of the ten Latin American decisions for war, eight were taken by Central American governments who went to war in 1885, 1906, and 1907 in a long-festering dispute over the past and potential union of Central American nations. These decisions fit theoretical expectations of closed domestic structures, low levels of foreign trade (given the small size of the economies), and generally lower levels of participation in limited-membership IGOs. The Pacific War between Bolivia and Chile does not fit the pattern with respect to foreign trade. Bolivia's economy was dominated by foreign-owned and -managed mining firms involved in the export of minerals, mostly through the ports annexed by Chile, which was also a major exporter of primary products. One can argue, therefore, that foreign trade concentrated in the export of a few primary products does not constrain decisions for war, especially in closed political systems that do not allow many private interests to influence policy.

The Spanish-American War (1898) over the independence of Cuba might also be classified as a Latin American war, but it clearly does not fit the Latin American pattern because Spain and the United States were rather open in domestic structure and more involved in international organization. Neither Spain nor the United States, however, can be considered to have possessed a large export sector, especially since the United States was in the middle third of traders because of the large size of its economy. Otherwise, it was the third-smallest trading nation, with exports only 7 percent of total output.

The Asian wars were marked by imperialistic ambitions; most

were initiated by Japan, which invaded China in 1894 and attacked Russia in 1904. In late August 1914, Japan also declared war on Germany in the hopes of furthering its territorial position in the Far East. As noted above, the rise of Japan is an interesting case for examination, since it generally contradicts the overall pattern and theoretical expectations. First, the constitution of 1890 gave Japan a parliamentary government that soon matched the authority of the emperor; political competition was extensive, although factional, and rival interests openly competed. Second, Japan's export sector grew rapidly, and this expansion did not seem to pose limitations on the use of force. As in the case of European great powers going to war in 1914, the Japanese decisions for war point to the unrestrained desire for expansion and security associated with power politics. The Sino-French War of 1884 was also imperialistic and contrary to expectations, because politically open, high-exporting, and IGO-intensive France went to war against closed, non-trading, IGO-averse China.

Table 8.1 does not show many distinct patterns of similarity between the governments that chose to fight against each other. Since over two-thirds of all governments were closed in this period, most wars were fought between governments with closed domestic structures. However, the Spanish-American War featured two comparatively open political systems, although Spain was much less democratic than the United States. The mixed cases are mostly imperialistic: France against China, Japan against China and later against Russia, and Spain against Morocco. The allied coalition in the Balkan Wars contained Serbia and Greece with open political systems, but also Bulgaria, Romania, and Turkey, which were closed. Similarly, the allied coalition against the Central Powers in World War I was mostly democratic, but also contained Russia.

There is greater similarity between belligerents on the dimension of foreign trade. Interestingly, five of the six mixed cases were wars of conquest: Russia against Turkey (1877), Chile against Bolivia (1879), France against China (1884), Italy against Turkey (1911), and Austria-Hungary against Serbia as the start of World War I. The exception is the United States and Spain in 1898, but it has already been noted that both were small exporters if economic size is not

175

taken into account. With the exception of Chile's attack of Bolivia, these are instances of more industrialized European powers expanding their empires at the expense of weaker governments.

Similarities between belligerents according to participation in limited-membership IGOs is notable, although easily understood as a result of the regional basis of warfare and international organization. Accordingly, the Asian and Balkan belligerents had few IGO memberships, Latin American belligerents had medium amounts, and the great powers had many memberships. Since IGO membership is not consistently related to decisions for war in this period, these similarities are not particularly enlightening.

In summary of the period before the First World War, the overall pattern fits the expectation that foreign trade acts as a constraint on war. The most important exception is the First World War itself, when large exporters decided to go to war in the first few weeks of August 1914. Unless the war is viewed more narrowly as a Balkan war, it stands out as evidence that security needs and the choice for war are not always constrained by foreign trading interests. The use of force and the need to protect vital security interests cannot be completely replaced by changing features of the global system; they can only be constrained by actors and interests who prefer other avenues of policy.

The twenty-four decisions for war in the 1919–39 period are displayed in table 8.2. Because economic data are not available for the belligerents in the two wars of 1919, these governments were categorized according to foreign-trade data in 1920. The pattern of distribution differs somewhat from the earlier period. With respect to domestic structure, eleven decisions for war (46%) were made by governments with open political systems. This is only slightly more than the distribution of open and closed domestic structures over the period (42% in 1920 and 38% in 1939). Governments of economies with larger foreign-trading sectors decided for war less often, but the relationship is weaker than in the pre–World War I era: eleven (46%) decisions by governments in the bottom third, seven (29%) by the middle third, and six (25%) by the top third. Unlike the previous period, however, participation in limited-membership IGOs is related to decisions for war: thirteen (54%) of belligerent governments are in the bottom third, seven (29%) in the middle,

TABLE 8.2 DECISIONS FOR WAR 1919–39, CATEGORIZED ACCORDING TO LEVELS OF TRADE, IGO PARTICIPATION, AND OPEN OR CLOSED POLITICAL SYSTEM

Low IGO Membership		Medium IGO Membership		High IGO Membership	
Closed	Open	Closed	Open	Closed	Open
Low Export					
Turkey '19		Greece '19	Poland '20		Paraguay '32
Hungary '19		Romania '19			
S. Africa '20					
S. Africa '39					
Poland '39					
Medium Export					
China '31	Finland '39		France '39	Italy '35	U.K. '39
Germany '39				Australia '39	
High Export					
	Czech. '19	Bolivia '32	Canada '39		
	Japan '31		New Zea.'39		
	Japan '37				
	S. Africa '39				

and only four (17%) in the top third. In short, the distribution of decisions for war matches the overall pattern for the pre–World War I era, but differences according to foreign trade are weaker, while differences in IGO membership are greater.

Although the European great powers of the nineteenth century exhibited common characteristics, the great powers of the interwar period are scattered across the categories at the time of their decisions for war. Germany and the Soviet Union were small traders with few IGO memberships. Japan was now a big trader, but had few IGO memberships. The United Kingdom and Italy were medium-level exporters, taking into account their economic size, and both were in the top third of IGO memberships. In a pronounced reversal from its position in 1914, the diminished size of the French export sector places it in the bottom third of exporters in 1939, with average participation in limited-membership IGOs. In contrast to the earlier period, when the great powers of Europe tended to share the characteristics of involvement in trade and IGOs, the interwar period shows striking diversity in the positions of the leading nations in world politics, which took one-third of the decisions for war in the period.

The six decisions for war taken in Eastern Europe in the post–World War I years of 1919 and 1920 fit the theoretical arguments most closely, with the exception of Czechoslovakia, which was democratic and export-oriented, although as a newly independent government not involved in international organization. Greece and Romania were older governments in 1919 and had more memberships in IGOs.

The other decisions for war in the interwar period are more complicated. In the 1871–1914 period, Japan's rising export sector did not constrain decisions for war, and shortly after World War I, Japan entered the top third of foreign-trading economies. By 1931, there were only four economies with a larger export sector than Japan's, reflecting both the rapid industrialization of Japan and the impact of global depression on the trading economies of the West. Since this analysis takes economic size into account, China's involvement in foreign trade is placed in the middle third, although in 1931 it was the fifth-smallest trader in absolute terms. Japan and China each had only one membership in a limited-membership IGO in 1931 and 1937. In all of Japan's decisions for war, we see evidence of unconstrained ambition and a tendency to use force. The role and influence of rival factions, especially the military, removed any potential constraint by foreign-trading interests.

The 1932 Chaco War between Paraguay and Bolivia does not fit the earlier pattern for Latin American wars. Bolivia was very export-oriented, although Paraguay was not. Both were members of many Pan-American international organizations, but both had closed political systems. Because economic data on Ethiopia is unavailable, it is only possible to report that Italy was in the middle third of trading nations and that it possessed many IGO memberships. Ethiopia, for its part, was not a member of any limited-membership IGOs, which befits an unindustrialized African nation in an era of colonialism. Both Italy and Ethiopia also had closed political systems.

World War II reflects both the theoretical argument of constraint and contradicts it. As in World War I, the two original belligerents, Germany and Poland, both were closed, small-trading, IGO-averse governments, if one does not control for economic size. However, when economic size is considered (see table 8.2), Germany is shown to have had a middle-range export sector. Democratic France and Great Britain quickly joined the war, and although the Depression adversely affected the French and British export sectors, they were bigger traders with many more connections to IGOs. Unlike the danger to Czechoslovakia in 1938, the apparent threats to security in 1939 overcame whatever constraint might have existed. The accompanying decisions by the Canadian, South African, Australian, and New Zealand governments show how traditional political relationships surpassed whatever principle or economic interest that argued against war. In examining the two world wars, which are defined by decisions for war by the most powerful nations of the day, there is evidence of the role of threat and power politics. The primacy of security is also revealed by the Soviet decision to attack Finland, which occurred later in 1939.

Similarities among the belligerents in this interwar era are few. With the exception of the Chaco War and the Italian invasion of Ethiopia, which were waged between closed governments, the wars of the interwar period involved governments with closed domestic political structures at war with open governments. Interestingly, because Japan's 1890 constitution was not undermined until after 1937, Japanese aggression in China reveals a comparatively open political system as aggressor. Besides Italy's invasion of Ethiopia, the other two wars of conquest were started by undemocratic governments, Germany and the Soviet Union, and waged against democracies, although in alliance with undemocratic Poland.

The interwar period is marked by greater diversity among the governments that chose to go to war, especially among the great powers. Further, closed political systems tended to fight against open ones. Involvement in foreign trade did not appear as a constraint, which may not be surprising given the depressed level of international commerce in a time of global economic downturn. Although the development of international organization was far advanced compared to earlier periods, it provided only a limited alternative to war. The inability of potential constraints on war to

179

TABLE 8.3 DECISIONS FOR WAR 1946–85, CATEGORIZED ACCORDING TO LEVELS OF TRADE, IGO PARTICIPATION, AND OPEN OR CLOSED POLITICAL SYSTEM

Low IGO Membership		Medium IGO Membership		High IGO Membership	
Closed	Open	Closed	Open	Closed	Open
Low Export					
Lebanon '48	Israel'48	Hungary '56	India '62	Argentina'82	Turkey '74
Jordan '48	Israel'56	U.S.S.R. '56	India '65	Uganda '78	
N. Korea '50		Egypt '73	Pakistan'65		
S. Korea '50			India '71		
P.R. China '62			Pakistan'71		
N. Vietnam '65					
S. Vietnam '65					
Syria '67					
Jordan '67					
Ethiopia '77					
N. Vietnam '78					
Cambodia '78					
Medium Export					
Somalia '77	Israel'67	Egypt '56	Egypt '48	Honduras'69	U.S. '50
	Israel'73	Egypt '67	Cyprus '74	Tanzania '78	France '56
					U.S. '65
					El Salvador'69
High Export					
Iraq '48		Iraq '80			U.K. '56
Syria '48		Iran '80			U.K. '82

operate in this era points out the enduring relevance of power politics and the requirements for security.

Table 8.3 arranges the forty-five decisions for war since 1945 according to levels of the three variables characteristic of constraint on decisions for war. In addition, the ten decisions for war since 1975 are included, even though the data is more speculative for some (especially Vietnam, Cambodia, Uganda, and Iran) and the categorization of trade involvement and participation in limited-membership IGOs is taken from 1975.

The distribution of decisions for war shown in table 8.3 summarizes the findings from earlier analyses. By dividing governments into three groups, it is again apparent that nations with high levels of trade are less likely to decide for war: twenty-five (56%) of the decisions for war were made by low traders, fourteen (33%) from the middle third, and only six (13%) from the group of high trading nations. These six decisions for war made by nations in the top third of trading nations stand out as exceptions to the findings that show trade is a constraint on decisions for war. Four of these decisions, by Iraq and Syria in 1948 and Iraq and Iran in 1980, were made by governments whose economies were dominated by single-commodity exports: oil in the case of Iran and Iraq, cotton in the case of Syria. In the nineteenth century, the exceptions to the trade constraint on war came from Latin American nations with large exports concentrated in a single or few primary products, which further confirms the hypothesis that the export constraint is qualified by the degree of concentration in export commodities, especially in primary products.

The United Kingdom comprises the outstanding exception to the constraint of foreign-trading involvement, because British trade is diversified among commodities and large even when the size of the economy is taken into account. Further, U.K. involvement in the Suez and the Falklands wars in the most recent period is matched by participation in both world wars of the twentieth century. In short, even though it is tempting to lessen the significance of the Suez and Falkland wars, which were both of relatively short duration and involved limited British casualties, the entire record of British war experience indicates that not every government faced by a large foreign-trading sector is constrained from the use of force. Perhaps governments with present or past great-power status must follow a different path of behavior in defense of imperial outposts, the symbolic or electoral value of which may be greater than prospective damage to a balance of trade. It can also be argued that the foreign-trade value of the Suez Canal is consistent with a primacy of economic interests in foreign policy, but an equivalent role for the Falkland Islands is hard to support. Finally, careful examination might reveal that the British political system is less open to the influence of private trading interests, especially if the rise of public enterprise lessens the influence of private commerce. However, government ownership of industry might otherwise strengthen economic priorities in government. If exceptions prove the rule, British decisions for war must be studied more closely.

Table 8.3 also shows that governments that are lesser participants in limited-membership international organizations tend to be more inclined to decide to war. However, this relationship is less profound than that for foreign trade: nineteen (43%) decisions for war were made by governments in the lowest third of membership, fifteen (33%) in the middle third, and eleven (24%) in the upper third. Although this is not a particularly strong relationship, it indicates that participation in limited-membership organizations can pose a constraint.

The distinction between open and closed political systems does not emerge as a constraint on decisions for war. Of the decisions shown in table 8.3 eighteen (40%) were by governments classified as open. Since 30 percent of the governments in this period are open, this is a somewhat larger percentage and consistent with the relationships found in chapter 6. Seven of the eighteen decisions (39%) for war by open governments are found among the governments most involved in limited-membership IGOs. Open political systems are thus potentially less constrained by membership in such organizations.

One-third of post–World War II decisions for war were taken by the Middle Eastern belligerents involved in the four Arab-Israeli Wars (1948, 1956, 1967, and 1973). With the previously noted exceptions of Iraq and Syria in 1948, the decisions meet the theoretical expectation, except that Egypt is a medium trader that moves into the lower third and that Israel is democratic and moves from the lower to middle third of trading nations. Only Egypt is in the middle third of IGO memberships. The two European belligerents in the 1956 Suez War, France and the United Kingdom, contradict this pattern of Middle East wars.

U.S. participation in two Asian wars, Korea in 1950 and Indochina in 1965, is also exceptional. As a democratic, middle-level trading nation with extensive IGO participation, the United States does not fit the postwar pattern, even though the other belligerents do. The two Koreas and two Vietnams were closed political systems that did not trade or participate in IGOs.

The three wars in South Asia correspond to the constraint of foreign trade because the governments going to war (India in 1962, 1965, and 1971; Pakistan in 1965 and 1971, and the People's Republic of China in 1962) are in the bottom third of trading nations. India and Pakistan, however, both had open political systems at the time of war, and both participated in IGOs. In the case of the two Indo-Pakistan wars, we have examples of two comparatively open political systems at war with each other.

This is also true of the Turkish-Cyprus War (1974), but Cyprus was a middle-level trader and Turkey belonged to many limited-membership IGOs. The only other European war of this period more closely matches expectations, as the Soviet Union and Hungary were both closed and low-level trading nations.

In the late 1970s there were two wars in Africa, the first since Italy's invasion of Ethiopia in 1935. In 1977, Somalia and Ethiopia fought over the control of Ogaden; both nations were undemocratic and had few IGO memberships. Ethiopia was a low-level trader, but Somalia was in the middle range. The 1978 war between Uganda and Tanzania is more of an exception, because both governments belonged to many limited-membership IGOs. Both had closed political systems and Tanzania was a middle-level trader.

Of the three periods examined here, patterns are strongest in the period since 1945, although there are interesting exceptions. As with findings reported earlier, foreign trade is revealed as the most consistent constraint on decisions for war. Such a finding appears more strongly when the size of national economies is not used as a factor in making comparisons. Accordingly, the large industrialized economies are generally found as exceptions to the theoretical expectations of this study.

CONCLUSIONS

In the opening chapters of this book, explanations of war based on the traditional and unchanging practice of power politics were juxtaposed against theoretical arguments positing that elemental transformations have altered the bases of international interaction. If the trends examined here were not found to be related to decisions for war, then it would be possible to conclude that the power-politics position of the constancy of international politics is the correct one. On the other hand, if the trends subjected to comparison with decisions for war accurately discriminated between governments going to war and those remaining at peace, then the findings would support the belief that the politics of war and peace are sensitive to the changing environment of domestic politics and international interactions.

The analyses presented here offer evidence for the latter position. Changing trends in interactions more broadly reflective of relations between independent governments than security interests alone have been shown empirically to be related to decisions for war. More importantly, the theoretical arguments advanced to justify their inclusion in an investigation of change in the global system have successfully guided the analyses to meaningful conclusions. In other words, sound arguments buttress empirical relationships that are evidence of the relevance of changing factors to decisions for war. The findings of this study cast doubt upon the usefulness of relying solely on power-politics explanations of why nations wage war.

First, the most consistent finding is the negative relationship between exports as a share of national output and decisions for war. National governments of economies that are proportionately more involved in export activity are less inclined to wage war. This is consistent with the trilogy of potential constraints on the use of force developed in chapter 2: interdependence increases the costs of waging war, interpenetration supports strong trading interests that may be injured by war, and interconnection of national economies reflects how the structure of government changes to incorporate commercial interests alongside security concerns.

Second, domestic political structure does not seem to be directly related to decisions for war. There is no difference, simply on the basis of executive authority and political competition, between national governments deciding for war and those remaining at peace. The particular issue over which wars are fought does have important implications. Specifically, governments with little political participation are prone to wage wars of conquest—wars in which the rights or resources of other governments are to be taken away. Wars of legitimacy—wars fought over a disagreement of rights or principles of conduct—tend to be waged by governments with more open domestic political structures. This is consistent with the notion that a national government requires a "legitimate" cause for war if it depends on maintaining broadly based political support. It also suggests that war is a policy that may be used for the domestic political ends of ruling elites. These relationships are not considered part of the lore of power politics. In fact, domestic political concerns are explicitly excluded from consideration, since the game of international politics precludes the interference of non-security political interests.

Perhaps more importantly, the relevance of issues in dispute indicates the importance of resolving disputes about legitimate rights of governments as a means to avoid interstate conflict. This finding supports the observation that if governments and international organizations were more successful at resolving such issues, war would undoubtedly be easier to avoid.

Another important finding concerns the cumulative effect of foreign trade and open domestic structures. In the presence of greater degrees of *both*, national governments are less likely to decide for war. It is in nations where the pacifistic inclinations of foreign traders can effectively influence policy through participation in government actions that more open political systems lead to constraints on decisions for war. Only when domestic interests opposed to war have effective means of influencing the actions of government does constraint exist.

A final set of findings pertains to the growth of international institutions as a rival to bilateral diplomatic interaction. Interestingly, only participation in limited-membership IGOs has a negative relationship to decisions for war, but only weakly so and only since 1919. This finding—that governments that conduct a greater portion of their international dealings through these organizations are less inclined to wage war—is consistent with the arguments advanced by functionalists, integrationists, and regionalists, who have suggested that a common interest in multilateral collaboration is sufficiently strong also to bind governments to peaceful relations.

The most important—although not unique—conclusion of this study, then, is that domestic and international political phenomena are important determinants of the foreign-policy actions of governments. What is perhaps unique, however, is the empirical evidence

185

that supports such a contention. The lore of power politics precludes the importance of socioeconomic change to the actions of independent governments in international politics and depicts diplomacy as a specialized science or peculiar art not to be understood in terms of general aspects of political life, but only in the context of relations between governments. The generalizations characteristic of theories derived from the power-politics perspective require such simplifications, but the findings described here suggest that they can be misleading.

These results call for two additional tasks. First, the influence of socioeconomic change must be incorporated into theoretical explanations of the causes of war. Second, further analyses are necessary to comprehend more fully the specific features of the relation of socioeconomic change to decisions for war.

The central focus has been on change in the global system and its effect on war. To this end, several additional conclusions can be drawn.

With reference to foreign trade, consistently strong and negative relationships exist since 1871, except for the interwar period. This finding poses the possibility that foreign trade has been a contributor to peace far longer than anticipated, but it is difficult to make a definitive statement regarding earlier periods of the global system. It is possible, for example, that the relationship of trade to war is present only in such periods of economic prosperity and growing foreign trade as those before 1914 and after 1945.

The nature of issues over which wars are waged is also indicative of change in international politics. Recent wars have largely been fought over the rights of governments and principles of conduct between governments. In fact, since World War II, no war of overt conquest has occurred. Because governments with open political structures are more prone to fight wars of legitimacy, political openness is increasingly related to decisions for war. Hence the use of foreign disputes to achieve domestic political ends may be a tendency worthy of further examination.

Finally, the relationship of participation in limited-membership IGOs is present only since 1919. It is therefore possible that sufficient commitment to international institutions has yet to be reached and that much more involvement in multilateral organizations may be necessary before greater inroads in the ability of governments to wage war are made.

Finally, the findings suggest that security interests may not be the ultimate preoccupation of the national governments. It seems, increasingly so over time, that other interests rival security in the priorities of government policy. In particular, foreign trade, economic growth, and domestic political considerations are related to decisions for war. Although these matters may have a direct bearing on the security of the nation, they are not associated with the lore of power politics and a narrow definition of security interests.

Considering the development of so much international interaction in non-security issues, it seems reasonable to conjecture that for many governments, possible threats to security are less important than several other policy goals. The small size of the military establishments of many contemporary governments is a testament to this tendency. The movement of non-aligned nations and the interest by many governments in a new international economic order are indicative of a change toward a greater concern for issues over which the use of force is less conceivable. Such a change marks a significant transformation of the global political system, one that projects optimism over the ability to avoid wars between independent governments in the future.

Further, issues of security are interdependent with other areas of transnational interaction. For example, policies and decisions dealing with security matters are influenced by certain features of foreign trade. Similarly, foreign trade is affected by the politics of defense and security. Although this study has focused exclusively on the relation of non-traditional factors to war, it suggests that the study of such linkages is likely to benefit the understanding of several other aspects of politics and economics. Specifically, in better assessing the linkage of foreign-trading interests to government, not only are the politics of war and peace better understood, but the politics of international commerce and the stakes, priorities, and bargaining capabilities of the government in managing trade.

This complication of theory rests on what may be the two underlying forms of behavior in the global system. On the one hand, governments clearly intend to *influence* the behavior of other governments. The tools and methods used to affect behavior modification in the international system are quite diverse, but can be reduced to the identification of influence-attempts and the evaluation of their success. This is the preoccupation of power-politics explanations, which emphasize how security depends on the extension of power, defined as the ability to compel one's will upon another. On the other hand, however, the politics of *management* of transnational relations takes place outside the realm of traditional modes of diplomatic interaction. Such dealings are political, in that they pertain to the distribution of global resources, but are based on the mutual and reciprocal bargaining intended to achieve routinized "regimes" of interaction—a sort of international public policy (see Keohane and Nye, 1977, chap. 2). The results of this study indicate that decisions for war do not pertain exclusively to influence-oriented politics and contain some degree of management-oriented politics as well.

In addition to the broadening of analytical perspectives by the consideration of more factors of a management nature, it also seems important to identify *constraints* as well as inducements to decisions for war. Instead of restricting analyses to the opportunities presented by the use of force, it is necessary at the same time to weigh the costs and tradeoffs associated with such actions. Potential gains by the use of force are easy to identify in almost any social situation. But what makes its use feasible in given circumstances separates opportunities from occurrences. Taken together, they are the necessary two sides of the same coin—the inducements motivating action and the constraints limiting it to feasible situations.

By expanding the conceptual material necessary fully to understand decisions for war, it is possible to summarize the implications of the research presented here. First, the treatment of decisions for war as part of the policy-making functions of national governments implies that foreign policy is but one objective on a public-policy agenda. Foreign policy must accordingly be understood in the context of domestic politics. After all, the same individuals responsible for foreign policy conduct the many other affairs of government. By approaching international politics in this manner, the complication of explanations of the causes of war by the incorporation of non-power-politics factors, management aspects of global politics, and the counterposition of inducements and constraints can be organized and still focused on the politics of war and peace.

THREE QUESTIONS ON THE CAUSES OF WAR

This book began by introducing a framework on the causes of war derived from the writings of Karl von Clausewitz, whose "trinity" of components forms the basis of decisions for war. Further, a critical distinction was made between volitional and environmental dimensions of the decisions for war. The result is a configuration of three distinct questions, the answers to all three of which are necessary for a complete theory of the causes of war.

First, a complete theory must identify the nature of disputes suitable to the use of force: Of all interactions between national societies, what types of disagreements suggest the use of force? Disputes over territory are one such disagreement, and the desire of governments to expand territory can serve as the basis of theory derived from the lore of power politics. Beyond aggression, what can be said of the nature of disputes that lie at the base of decisions for war? In this study, the broad category of disputes over legitimacy, defined as the rights and conduct of governments, contains far too many issues to be summarized neatly.

Because this question directs attention to the troublesome issue of motivations in foreign policy, an easy answer is impossible. A volitional perspective suggests that governments are in a position to construct goals for action and design strategies to achieve them. To a limited extent, this may be true, but a strong case can also be made that goals for government are produced by its environment in the form of demands and pressures to satisfy the needs of a population. The question then becomes: Whence come goals for government? In the end, the identification of motivations rests with the ability to understand the relationship between government and the people. Unfortunately for the building of a theory of the causes of war, this relationship is quite distinct for each government and difficult to generalize. Moreover, it is a dynamic relationship that evolves with the ever-changing socioeconomic fabric of society.

Since government exists as a distinct actor in a domestic political system, it is possible to assert that government will acquire an autonomous set of goals that are not merely the consequence or summary of the dominant interests in society. But since government rests on some form of political legitimacy, defined as the requirements of rule, these goals cannot be too far detached from society. To balance the volitional and environmental dimensions of disputes underlying war, it is necessary to balance the interests and goals of government against the demands and pressures of a society. The answer is provided by the study of state-society relations and cannot come from the lore of power politics, which avoids such issues.

The second question involves the calculation of the chances for success: How do governments evaluate the prospects for success in the use of force? The environmental determinants of power in the global system provide much of the answer. However, the translation of power potential into military capabilities to be used in wartime requires the action of government. To the extent that governments have the opportunity to prepare for particular military contingencies, a volitional dimension of the prospects for success arises. Thus, a smaller or weaker government can expect to have success against a potentially larger foe, if even in a limited or confined instance.

The choice of strategies and the maintenance of military establishments is not a simple endeavor. Security policy must always reflect a compromise between security goals and what burden a society will bear to support peacetime and wartime military forces. In short, the domestic political system exists as the environment that poses real limitations on government's ability to prepare for military actions.

The third question is the most important, if only because our ability to answer it holds the key to understanding war: When do governments choose to use force to compel their will on another government? The volitional dimension is derived from the choice to pursue certain goals (the answer to the first question) with the military capabilities deemed sufficient (the answer to the second). The matching of means to ends produces the Clausewitzian observation that war is the pursuit of policy. The environmental dimension is equally important and comprises all the constraints and inducements to such a choice. Although this study has identified several potential areas of constraint, this question is too complicated to be answered simply by constructing an inventory of stimuli and limitations on the use of force.

Theories that build upon the lore of power politics can provide an answer to this question, even if it appears in a general form: the choice for war is made when the threat to a government's security is sufficiently great or when the potential gain to security is sufficiently large as to warrant the use of force. But this answer is far too general; in particular, it cannot treat the variety of goals for government that serve as the issues underlying disputes leading to war.

If we see the motivations for war as arising from the intersection of government and societal interests—in other words, state-society relations—then it is possible to a formulate a different, if equally general answer to the question of when governments decide for war. By recognizing a prominent role for state-society relations, the decision to use force can be identified with threats to the tenure of office of ruling elites. Naturally, this would include external threats in the form of occupation or displacement by rival governments. In this way, power politics and the security of the nation has a place in the explanation of decisions for war. However, the use of force can also satisfy the needs of ruling elites that find it difficult to resolve contentious domestic rivalries or to accomplish goals established by society. The choice for war can thus arrive when a government faces direct foreign challenge, but also when it finds that its tenure in office can be extended by mobilizing society for war.

The opportunity to choose war as a government policy, then, rests on the configuration of political interests that will either gain or lose as a result of a decision for war. Investigations into the constraints on decisions for war is necessary. This study has identified foreign-trading interests as manifested by an economy's involvement in foreign trade as a potent constraint, even if there are important qualifications. For example, the exceptional cases of Britain's wars over the Suez Canal and the Falklands can be seen as sufficiently important to the electoral prospects of the British government as to override the constraints posed by rival political elites.

In the end, the matching of the goals of government to decisions for war is a complicated task and one that leads inevitably to Clausewitz's observation on the chameleon-like character of war.

An important part of the understanding of the causes of war rests in the recognition that theories will be somewhat tentative and subject to constant revision. Therefore, we should focus our attention on the enduring and theoretically meaningful questions, knowing that we must continually improve the quality of our answers. Some measure of satisfaction can be taken from scholarship that already provides answers, but theory is never complete, and additional research can serve only to build better answers for the future.

REFERENCES

Aldcroft, Derek H. 1981. *From Versailles to Wall Street*. Berkeley: University of California Press.

Altfeld, Michael, and Bruce Bueno de Mesquita. 1979. "Choosing Sides in Wars." *International Studies Quarterly* 23/1, pp. 87–112.

Angell, Robert. 1969. *Peace on the March: Transnational Participation*. New York: Van Nostrand Reinhold.

Bairoch, Paul. 1975. *The Economic Development of the Third World since 1900*. Berkeley: University of California Press.

———. 1976. *Commerce exterieur et developpement economique de l'Europe au XIX siècle*. Paris: Ecole des hautes études en sciences sociales.

———. 1976. "Europe's Gross National Product, 1800–1974." *Journal of European Economic History* 5 (Fall), pp. 273–340.

Baldwin, David A. 1979. "Power Analysis and World Politics: New Trends versus Old Tendencies." *World Politics* 31, pp. 161–94.

Banks, Arthur. 1977. *Political Handbook of the World*. New York: McGraw Hill.

Barry, Brian. 1970. *Sociologists, Economists, and Democracy*. London: Macmillan.

Bastiat, Frederic. 1922. *Economic Sophism*. Trans. P. J. Stirling. New York: G. P. Putnam's Sons.

Bentham, Jeremy. 1843. "A Manual of Political Economy." In John Bowring (ed.), *Bentham's Works*. Edinburgh: Tait.

Berger, Suzanne (ed.). 1981. *Organizing Interests in Western Europe: Pluralism, Corporatism, and the Transformation of Politics*. Cambridge: Cambridge University Press.

Blechman, Barry M., and Stephen S. Kaplan. 1978. *Force without War: U.S. Armed Forces as a Political Instrument*. Washington: Brookings Institution.

Brodie, Bernard. 1973. *War and Politics*. New York: Macmillan.

Bueno de Mesquita, Bruce. 1985. *The War Trap*. New Haven: Yale University Press.

———. 1985. "The War Trap Revisited." *American Political Science Review* 79/1 (March), pp. 156–77.

Bullock, Alan, and Maurice Shock (eds.). 1956. *The Liberal Tradition: From Fox to Keynes.* Oxford: Clarendon.

Butterworth, Robert L. 1978. *Moderation from Management: International Organizations and Peace.* Pittsburgh: University Center for International Studies, University of Pittsburgh.

Buzan, Barry. 1984. "Economic Structure and International Security: The Limits of the Liberal Case." *International Organization* 38/4 (Autumn), pp. 597–624.

Carr, Edward Hallett. 1939. *The Twenty Years' Crisis, 1919–1939.* London: Macmillan.

Chan, Steve. 1984. "Mirror, Mirror on the Wall . . . Are the Freer Countries More Pacific?" *Journal of Conflict Resolution* 27/1 (December), pp. 617–48.

Choucri, Nazli, and Robert C. North. 1975. *Nations in Conflict: National Growth and International Violence.* San Francisco: Freeman.

Clausewitz, Karl von. 1832. *On War.* London: Penguin, 1968.

Cobden, Richard. 1870. *Speeches by Richard Cobden.* London: Macmillan.

Cohen, Bernard C. 1973. *The Public's Impact on Foreign Policy.* Boston: Little, Brown.

Cooper, Richard N. 1968. *The Economics of Interdependence: Economic Policy in the Atlantic Community.* New York: McGraw Hill.

Craig, Gordon A., and Alexander L. George. 1983. *Force and Statecraft: Diplomatic Problems of Our Time.* New York: Oxford University Press.

Day, Alan J. 1982. *Border and Territorial Disputes.* Harlow, Essex: Longman.

Deutsch, Karl W., and Alexander Eckstein. 1961. "National Industrialization and the Declining Share of the International Sector, 1890–1959." *World Politics* 13/2 (January), pp. 267–99.

Deutsch, Karl W. 1961. "Social Mobilization and Political Development." *American Political Science Review* 55/3 (September), pp. 493–513.

Downs, George, and David Rocke. 1987. "Tacit Bargaining and Arms Control." *World Politics* 39/3 (April), pp. 297–325.

Durkheim, Emile. 1947. *The Division of Labor in Society.* Glencoe, Ill.: Free Press.

Eberwein, Wolf Dieter. 1981. "The Quantitative Study of International Conflict: Quantity and Quality?" *Journal of Peace Research* 18/1, pp. 19–38.

Fink, Clinton F. 1968. "Some Conceptual Difficulties in the Theory of Social Conflict." *Journal of Conflict Resolution* 12/4, pp. 412–60.

Finney, D. J. 1971. *Probit Analysis*. London: Cambridge University Press.

Flora, Peter, and Arnold J. Heidenheimer. 1981. "The Historical Core and Changing Boundaries of the Welfare State." In Flora and Heidenheimer (eds.), *The Development of Welfare States in Europe and America*. London: Transaction Books, pp. 17–36.

Gasiorowski, Mark J. 1986. "Economic Interdependence and International Conflict." *International Studies Quarterly* 30/1 (March), pp. 23–38.

Geiss, Imanuel. 1967. *July 1914: The Outbreak of the First World War*. New York: Charles Scribner's Sons.

Gilpin, Robert. 1975. *U.S. Power and the Multinational Corporation*. New York: Basic Books.

———. 1981. *War and Change in World Politics*. London: Cambridge University Press.

Gourevitch, Peter A. 1978. "The Second Image Reversed: The International Sources of Domestic Politics," *International Organization* 32/4 (Autumn), pp. 881–913.

Grotius. 1925. *The Law of War and Peace*. Oxford: Oxford University Press.

Gurr, Ted Robert. 1974. "Persistence and Change in Political Systems, 1800–1971." *American Political Science Review* 68/4 (December), pp. 1482–1504.

———. 1978. *Comparative Studies of Political Conflict and Change: Cross National Datasets* Ann Arbor: Inter-university Consortium for Political and Social Research.

Haas, Ernst B., Robert L. Butterworth, and Joseph S. Nye. 1972. *Conflict Management by International Organizations*. Morristown, N.J.: General Learning Press.

Haas, Ernst B. 1953. "The Balance of Power as a Guide to Policy-Making." *Journal of Politics* 15 (August), pp. 370–98.

———. 1953. "The Balance of Power: Prescription, Concept or Propaganda?" *World Politics* 5 (July), pp. 442–77.

———. 1958. *The Uniting of Europe*. Stanford: Stanford University Press.

———. 1964. *Beyond the Nation-State: Functionalism and International Organization* Stanford: Stanford University Press.

———. 1983. "Regime Decay: Conflict Management and International Organizations, 1945–1981." *International Organization* 37/2 (Spring), pp. 189–256.

Hanson, John R., II. 1980. *Trade in Transition: Exports from the Third World, 1840–1900*. New York: Academic Press.

Hanushek, Eric A., and John E. Jackson. 1977. *Statistical Methods for Social Scientists.* New York: Academic Press.

Hardach, Gerd. 1977. *The First World War, 1914–1918.* Berkeley: University of California Press.

Hemleben, Sylvester John. 1943. *Plans for World Peace through Six Centuries.* Chicago: University of Chicago Press.

Hilgerdt, Folke. 1945. *Industrialization and Foreign Trade.* Geneva: League of Nations, Financial and Transit Department.

Hinsley, F. H. 1963. *Power and the Pursuit of Peace: Theory and Practice in the History of Relations between States.* Cambridge: Cambridge University Press.

Hirschman, Albert O. 1945. *National Power and the Structure of Foreign Trade.* Berkeley: University of California Press.

Hobbes, Thomas. 1946. *Leviathan.* Oxford: Basil Blackwell.

Hoffmann, Stanley. 1973. "The Acceptability of Military Force." *Force in Modern Societies: Its Place in International Politics.* London: International Institute for Strategic Studies, Adelphi Paper Number 102.

Howard, Michael. 1961. *The Franco-Prussian War: The German Invasion of France, 1870–71.* New York: Macmillan.

———. 1972. "Changes in the Use of Force, 1919–1969." In Brian Porter (ed.), *The Aberystwyth Papers: International Politics, 1919–1969.* London: Oxford University Press.

Inglehart, Ronald. 1977. *The Silent Revolution: Changing Values and Political Styles in Western Publics.* Princeton: Princeton University Press.

International Institute for Strategic Studies. *Strategic Survey.* London: International Institute for Strategic Studies, various editions.

Jacobson, Harold K. 1979. *Networks of Interdependence: International Organizations and the Global Political System.* New York: Knopf.

Jacobson, Harold K., William M. Reisinger, and Todd Mathers. 1986. "National Entanglements in International Governmental Organizations." *American Political Science Review* 80/1, pp. 141–59.

Jervis, Robert. 1976. *Perception and Misperception in International Politics.* Princeton: Princeton University Press.

Katzenstein, Peter J. 1976. "International Relations and Domestic Structures: Foreign Economic Policies of Advanced Industrial States." *International Organization* 30/1 (Winter), pp. 1–45.

Kennan, George F. 1955. *Realities of American Foreign Policy.* Princeton: Princeton University Press.

Keohane, Robert O., and Joseph S. Nye. 1977. *Power and Interdependence: World Politics in Transition.* Boston: Little, Brown.

Keohane, Robert O. 1983. "Theory of World Politics: Structural Realism and Beyond." In Ada W. Finifter (ed.), *Political Science: The State of the Discipline.* Washington: American Political Science Association, pp. 503–40.

———. 1984. *After Hegemony: Cooperation and Discord in the World Political Economy.* Princeton: Princeton University Press.

Kindleberger, Charles P. 1978. "The Rise of Free Trade." *Economic Response: Comparative Studies in Trade, Finance, and Growth.* Cambridge: Harvard University Press.

Kissinger, Henry A. 1978. "The Lessons of the Past." *The Washington Review* 1/1 (January), pp. 3–9.

Kmenta, Jan. 1971. *Elements of Econometrics.* New York: Macmillan.

Knorr, Klaus, and James N. Rosenau (eds.). 1969. *Contending Approaches to International Politics.* Princeton: Princeton University Press.

Kohl, Juergen. 1983. "The Functional Structure of Public Expenditures: Long-Term Changes." In Charles Lewis Taylor (ed.), *Why Governments Grow: Measuring Public Sector Size.* Beverly Hills: Sage.

Krasner, Stephen D. 1978. *Defending the National Interest: Raw Materials Investments and U.S. Foreign Policy.* Princeton: Princeton University Press.

Kugler, Jacek, and William K. Domke. 1986. "The Strength of Nations." *Comparative Political Studies* (April) 19/1, pp. 39–69.

Kurth, James R. 1979. "The Political Consequences of the Product Cycle: Industrial History and Political Outcomes." *International Organization* 33/1, pp. 1–34.

Kuznets, Simon. 1966. *Modern Economic Growth: Rate, Structure and Spread.* New Haven: Yale University Press.

———. 1967. "Quantitative Aspects of the Foreign Economic Growth of Nations: X, Level and Structure of Foreign Trade, Long-Term Trends." *Economic Development and Cultural Change* 15 (January, part 2).

———. 1968. *Toward a Theory of Economic Growth.* New York: W. W. Norton.

Langer, William L. 1972. *Encyclopedia of World History.* Boston: Houghton Mifflin. Fifth edition.

Lauren, Paul Gordon. 1976. *Bureaucrats and Diplomats: The First Institutional Responses to Twentieth Century Diplomacy in France and Germany.* Stanford: Hoover Institution.

Leng, Russell J., and Charles S. Gochman. 1982. "Dangerous Disputes: A Study of Conflict Behavior and War." *American Journal of Political Science* 26/4 (November), pp. 664–87.

Leng, Russell J. 1983. "When Will They Ever Learn: Coercive Bargaining in Recurrent Crises." *Journal of Conflict Resolution* 27/3 (September), pp. 379–420.

Lerner, Daniel. 1956. "French Business Leaders Look at the EDC." *Public Opinion Quarterly* 20 (Spring).

Levy, Marion J., Jr. 1966. *Modernization and the Structure of Societies: A Setting for International Affairs.* Princeton: Princeton University Press.

Lijphart, Arend. 1974. "The Structure of the Theoretical Revolution in International Relations." *International Studies Quarterly* 18/1 (March), pp. 41–74.

Lindberg, Leon N., and Stuart A. Scheingold. 1970. *Europe's Would-be Polity: Patterns of Change in the European Community.* Englewood Cliffs: Prentice-Hall.

Luterbacher, Urs. 1984. "Last Words about War." *Journal of Conflict Resolution* 28/1 (March), pp. 165–82.

McNeill, William H. 1982. *The Pursuit of Power: Technology, Armed Force, and Society since A.D. 1000.* Chicago: University of Chicago Press.

Maddison, Angus. 1977. "Phases of Capitalist Development." *Banco Nazionale del Lavoro Quarterly Review* 12/1 (June), pp. 103–38.

Maghoori, Ray, and Bennett Ramberg. 1982. *Globalism versus Realism: International Relations' Third Debate.* Boulder: Westview.

Maizels, Alfred. 1963. *Industrial Growth and World Trade.* Cambridge: Cambridge University Press.

Mansbach, Richard, and John A. Vasquez. 1981. *In Search of Theory: A New Paradigm for World Politics.* New York: Columbia University Press.

Marx, Karl, and Friedrich Engels. 1955. *The Communist Manifesto.* New York: Appleton-Century-Crofts.

Maier, Charles S. 1977. "The Politics of Productivity: Foundations of American International Economic Policy after World War II." *International Organization* 31/4 (Autumn), pp. 23–50.

May, Ernest R. *American Imperialism.* New York: Atheneum, 1968.

Meinecke, Friedrich. 1957. *Machiavellism: The Doctrine of Raison d'Etat and Its Place in Modern History.* New Haven: Yale University Press.

Migdal, Joel S. 1983. "Studying the Politics of Development and Change: The State of the Art." In Ada W. Finifter (ed.), *Political Science: State of the Discipline.* Washington: American Political Science Association.

Mill, John Stuart. 1909. *Principles of Political Economy.* London: Longmans.

Milward, Alan S. 1979. *War, Economy and Society, 1939–1945*. Berkeley: University of California Press.

Mitrany, David. 1966. *A Working Peace System*. Chicago: Quadrangle.

Modelski, George. 1978. "The Long-Cycle of Global Politics and the Nation-State." *Comparative Studies in Society and History* 20, pp. 214–35.

Morgenthau, Hans J. 1948. *Politics among Nations*. New York: Knopf.

Morse, Edward. 1976. *Modernization and the Transformation of International Relations*. New York: Free Press.

Most, Benjamin A., and Harvey Starr. 1984. "International Relations Theory, Foreign Policy Substitutability, and 'Nice' Laws." *World Politics* 36/3 (April), pp. 383–406.

Mulhall, Michael G. 1898. "Commerce." In *Dictionary of Statistics*. London: George Routledge and Sons. Fourth edition.

Nicholson, Harold. 1954. *The Evolution of Diplomatic Method*. London: Constable & Co.

Nordlinger, Eric A. 1981. *On the Autonomy of the Democratic State*. Cambridge: Harvard University Press.

Nye, Joseph S. 1971. *Peace in Parts: Integration and Conflict in Regional Organization*. Boston: Little, Brown.

OECD (Organization for Economic Cooperation and Development). 1978. *Public Expenditure Trends*. Paris: OECD.

Olson, Mancur, Jr. 1968. *The Logic of Collective Action: Public Goods and the Theory of Groups*. New York: Schocken.

Organski, A. F. K. 1968. *World Politics*. New York: Knopf.

Organski, A. F. K., and Jacek Kugler. 1980. *The War Ledger*. Chicago: University of Chicago Press.

Polachek, Sol W. 1980. "Conflict and Trade." *Journal of Conflict Resolution* 24/1 (March), pp. 55–78.

Pollard, Sidney. 1981. *The Integration of the European Economy since 1815*. London: Allen and Unwin.

Polyani, Karl. 1944. *The Great Transformation: The Political and Economic Origins of Our Time*. Boston: Beacon.

Pryor, Frederic L. 1968. *Public Expenditures in Communist and Capitalist Nations*. Homewood, Ill.: Richard D. Irwin.

Richardson, Lewis Fry. 1960. *Statistics of Deadly Quarrels*. Pittsburgh: Boxwood.

Riker, William H. 1964. *Federalism: Origin, Operation, Significance*. Boston: Little, Brown.

Rittberger, Volker. 1973. *Evolution and International Organization: Toward a New Level of Sociopolitical Integration*. The Hague: Nijhoff.

Rokkan, Stein. 1975. "Dimensions of State Formation and Nation-Building: A Possible Paradigm for Research on Variations within Europe." In Charles Tilly (ed.), *The Formation of National States in Western Europe*. Princeton: Princeton University Press, pp. 562–600.

Rosecrance, Richard, and Arthur Stein. 1973. "Interdependence: Myth and Reality." *World Politics* 26/1 (October), pp. 1–27.

Rosecrance, Richard, et al. 1977. "Whither Interdependence." *International Organization* 31/3 (Summer), pp. 425–45.

Rousseau, Jean-Jacques. 1917. *A Lasting Peace through the Federation of Europe and the State of War*. London: Constable.

Ruggie, John Gerard. 1983. "Continuity and Transformation in the World Polity: Toward a Neo-Realist Synthesis." *World Politics* 35/2 (January), pp. 261–85.

Rummel, Rudolph. 1983. "Libertarianism and International Violence." *Journal of Conflict Resolution* 27 (March), pp. 27–71.

Russett, Bruce M., and Elizabeth Hanson. 1975. *Interest and Ideology: The Foreign Policy Beliefs of American Businessmen*. San Francisco: Freeman.

Russett, Bruce M., J. David Singer, and Melvin Small. 1968. "National Political Units in the Twentieth Century: A Standardized List." *American Political Science Review* 62/3 (September), pp. 932–51.

Russett, Bruce M. 1967. *International Regions and the International System: A Study in Political Ecology*. Chicago: Rand McNally.

Sartori, Giovanni. 1976. *Parties and Party Systems: A Framework for Analysis*. Cambridge: Cambridge University Press.

Silberner, Edmund. 1946. *The Problem of War in Nineteenth Century Economic Thought*. Princeton: Princeton University Press.

Singer, J. David, and Michael D. Wallace. 1970. "International Governmental Organization and the Preservation of Peace, 1816–1964: Some Bivariate Relationships." *International Organization* 24 (Summer).

Singer, J. David, and Melvin Small. 1972. *The Wages of War*. New York: Wiley.

Singer, J. David. 1981. "Accounting for International War: The State of the Discipline." *Journal of Peace Research* 18/1, pp. 1–18.

Siverson, Randolph M., and Michael P. Sullivan. 1983. "The Distribution of Power and the Onset of War." *Journal of Conflict Resolution* 27/3 (September), pp. 463–94.

Small, Melvin, and J. David Singer. 1976. "The War-Proneness of Democratic Regimes, 1816–1965." *Jerusalem Journal of International Relations* 1/1, pp. 40–68.

———. 1982. *Resort to Arms: International and Civil Wars, 1816–1980.* Beverly Hills: Sage.

Smith, Adam. 1776. *The Wealth of Nations.* Chicago: University of Chicago Press, 1976.

Snyder, Glenn H., and Paul Diesing. 1977. *Conflict among Nations: Bargaining, Decision-making and System Structure in International Crises.* Princeton: Princeton University Press.

Sprout, Harold, and Margaret Sprout. 1965. *The Ecological Perspective on Human Affairs: With Special Reference to International Politics.* Princeton: Princeton University Press.

Sutherland, Gillian. 1972. *Studies in the Growth of Nineteenth-century Government.* Totowa, N.J.: Rowman and Littlefield.

Taagepera, Rein. 1976. "Why the Trade/GNP Ratio Decreases with Country Size." *Social Science Research* 5.

Tashjean, John E. 1986. "Clausewitz: Naval and Other Considerations." *Naval War College Review* 39/3 (May–June), pp. 51–58.

Taylor, Charles Lewis, and Michael C. Hudson. 1972. *World Handbook of Political and Social Indicators.* New Haven: Yale University Press.

Thucydides. 1954. *History of the Peloponnesian War.* London: Penguin.

Tilly, Charles. 1975. "Reflections on the History of European State Making." In Tilly (ed.), *The Formation of National States in Western Europe.* Princeton: Princeton University Press, pp. 3–83.

Ulam, Adam. 1968. *Expansion and Coexistence: The History of Soviet Foreign Policy, 1917–1967.* New York: Praeger.

Viner, Jacob. 1948. "Power versus Plenty as Objectives of Foreign Policy in the 17th and 18th Centuries." *World Politics* 1/1 (October), pp. 1–29.

Wagner, R. Harrison. 1984. "War and Expected-Utility Theory." *World Politics* 36/3 (April), pp. 407–23.

Wallace, Michael, and J. David Singer. 1970. "Intergovernmental Organization and the Preservation of Peace, 1816–1964." *International Organization* 24, pp. 520–47.

Waltz, Kenneth N. 1959. *Man, the State and War.* New York: Columbia University Press.

———. 1970. "The Myth of National Interdependence." In Charles P. Kindleberger (ed.), *The International Corporation.* Cambridge: MIT Press, pp. 205–23.

———. 1979. *Theory of International Politics.* Reading, Mass.: Addison-Wesley.

Weber, Max. 1947. *The Theory of Social and Economic Organization.* Trans.

A. M. Henderson and Talcott Parsons. London: Oxford University Press.

Weede, Erich. 1984. "Democracy and War Involvement." *Journal of Conflict Resolution* 28/4 (December), pp. 649–64.

Weisberg, Herbert F. 1974. "Models of Statistical Relationship." *American Political Science Review* 68/4 (December), pp. 1638–55.

Wight, Martin. 1946. *Power Politics*. London: Royal Institute of International Affairs. Revised and edited posthumously by Hedley Bull and Carsten Holbraad. Leicester: Leicester University Press, 1978.

Wilkenfeld, Jonathan. 1972. "Models for the Analysis of Foreign Conflict Behavior of States." In Bruce M. Russett (ed.), *Peace, War and Numbers*. Beverly Hills: Sage.

Wilson, Woodrow. 1927. *The Public Papers of Woodrow Wilson: War and Peace*. Ray S. Baker and William E. Dodd (eds.). New York: Harper and Brothers.

Wolfers, Arnold. 1959. "Actors in International Politics." In William T. R. Fox (ed.), *Theoretical Aspects of International Relations*. South Bend: University of Notre Dame Press, pp. 83–106.

———. 1962. "The Pole of Power and the Pole of Indifference." In *Discord and Collaboration: Essays on International Politics*. Baltimore: Johns Hopkins Press, pp. 81–102.

Woodruff, William. 1973. "The Emergence of an International Economy, 1700–1914." In Carlo M. Cipolla (ed.), *The Fontana Economic History of Europe: Volume IV, The Emergence of Industrial Societies, Part II*. Glasgow: William Collins, pp. 675–77.

World Bank. 1983. *World Development Report 1983*. New York: Oxford University Press.

Wright, Quincy. 1942. *A Study of War*. Chicago: Chicago University Press.

———. 1965. "The Escalation of International Conflicts." *Journal of Conflict Resolution* 9/4, pp. 434–49.

Zacher, Mark W. 1979. *International Conflicts and Collective Security, 1946–1977*. New York: Praeger.

Zimmerman, L. J. 1962. "The Distribution of World Income, 1860–1960." In Egbert de Vries (ed.), *Essays on Unbalanced Growth*. The Hague: Mouton, pp. 28–55.

INDEX